AF579077

Man on the Run

At the age of fifteen he signed on at the Dell,
All the Saints fans soon knew him well.
Wembley, 1976,
And little Bobby Stokes hit United for six.
They held the Cup high, their medals too,
But then Mick Channon was to start anew.

Off up the motorway to Manchester City.
Oh what a pity, the two years at City
Did not work out very well,
But as time would tell,
It was not long till he was back at the Dell.

Although very keen, the goals became lean,
So off with a song he soon was gone,
And on the Canary scene,
Wearing yellow and green.

Now he's at Pompey,
Not quite a donkey,
For they haven't put him out to grass.
After all that's past,
The fans wonder how he can last.
They are not bored,
For he has just scored.

Michael Channon Jnr, *8 January 1986*

MAN ON THE RUN

Mick Channon

ARTHUR BARKER LIMITED
A subsidiary of Weidenfeld (Publishers) Limited

Illustrations by Don Osmond (Oz)

Published in Great Britain by
Arthur Barker Limited
91 Clapham High Street
London SW4 7TA

ISBN 0 213 16930 4

Printed in Great Britain by
Butler & Tanner Ltd
Frome and London

Contents

Acknowledgements

I would like to give special thanks to sports journalist, Ian Gibb, for his support and expertise. His friendly help and understanding have made it a pleasure for me to write about my experiences.

Illustrations

The photographs in this book are produced by the kind permission of Syndication International unless otherwise stated.

1 · Early Days

It all started for me in a little place called Orcheston on Salisbury Plain. I certainly didn't come from a footballing background: it was more of a breeding ground for farming folk. At junior school I didn't even have a football team. It was at Amesbury Secondary School – a seven-mile bus ride from home – that I started to play the game. I knew I was fairly good and would play in every spare minute of the day. But there was no great family support at that stage, my father was probably more interested in showjumping. But he would have a kick-about like most fathers do with their sons. To be fair to him, he used to work all the hours that God sends and didn't have that much free time. As a civil servant in the War Department at Larkhill he would be away for long spells and I often didn't see him until the end of the week.

My dad would watch me play on a Saturday morning and, perhaps once a month, take me to watch Southampton's games. I was lucky, I came from a good home. I was one of three brothers, John the eldest, then me and the youngest Phil. The death of John, when he was fourteen, in a tractor accident had a profound effect on me. I was nearly ten when it happened. John's death is something I can never forget, mostly for the great sadness it caused at home. I can still vividly remember my mother often sobbing to herself.

My dad was working in his holidays for a local farmer and John was helping out. He was almost fifteen and just trying to earn a few quid. They were harvesting, and at about tea-time I would usually find out where they were and ride over on my bike to see them. I remember riding down to the house of a family friend, Mrs Walters, and asking where Dad and John were working. I would take their tea up to them. I'll never forget it, I went to the door and she said: 'Michael, is your mum in?' I knew there was something wrong immediately. I was hustled off to my gran's about five o'clock. It wasn't until gone ten that my aunty took me back home and mum told me that John had been killed. I remember crying. Phil was only five and too young to understand. But what hurt me most, and hit me for months and years afterwards, was hearing my mother cry.

There was a terrible sadness, knowing there was nothing I could do. I think that's why religiously I've been a non-believer ever since. I want to believe in God, but that tragedy is one of the reasons I can't. However, I haven't brought up my kids, Nicola and Michael, that way. I've left it to them to decide because I think religion is very much a personal choice. Everything is there for them when they are old enough and wise enough to make their own decisions.

John loved his bikes and I remember the times he used to send me off home. Like any kid, he didn't want his younger brother around if he could later tell tales on him.

Back in 1959, when the accident happened, there wasn't half of the safety knowledge there is today. John was driving a tractor down a hill with a load of bales of hay on it. The trailer turned over. A couple of other lads on the tractor managed to jump clear. But my brother was trapped in the driver's seat when the tractor tipped over as well and crushed him.

After that I threw myself into my football as much as I could to take my mind off the tragedy. I played for Amesbury Secondary Modern up to under-15s, for Salisbury and District and then for Wiltshire. It was at County level that I was spotted by Southampton.

I played at Andover for Wiltshire against Hampshire and although we lost 5–3 I scored twice. The then Swindon

Town manager, Bert Head, wanted to sign me and was going to come down to see me after the Wednesday on which I'd played. However, first to arrive was Southampton's manager, Ted Bates, who turned up on the Sunday.

Southampton's chief scout, Tom Parker, formerly of Arsenal and England, met my dad and me before taking me to my digs, which were within walking distance of the ground. Mrs Fyfe was my landlady at 40 Wilton Avenue. Lodging with me were Gerry Gurr, who was a decent goal-keeper, and Tony Byrne, a better golfer than footballer. He certainly spent more time on the golf course than he did playing football. Tony was a real Cockney character. There were about seven people living at that house, not all of them footballers. They were hard times – but good times.

I was earning £7 a week, the average wage for an apprentice in 1964, and out of that I had to pay £4.50 for my digs. That doesn't happen today, the apprentice has his digs already paid for with his £50-a-week wages on top. So by the time my national insurance was taken out I probably had two quid for the week – a far cry from becoming the best paid player in England on over £1,000-a-week basic! Back in 1964 I suppose £2 was quite a bit of cash, like a tenner today.

Football then seemed a marvellous career for the likes of me, not the brightest lad in school. The only real education I've had is in life – and I like to think I've got an 'A' level in that. Playing football; being with some right herberts; and living off my wits – that, basically, is what the growing Mick Channon was all about.

It was a choice of football, farm work, which most of the local lads went into from where I came from, or going into the army. There was no easy way out for a country boy with a broad Wiltshire accent like me. I like to think I would still have made something of my life, even without football, but like everything else you need the rub of the green along the way. In life you get the odd break and it really all depends on how you take it. The opportunity is there – it's how you handle it that counts.

So now I was an apprentice, living with seven other lads and frightened to take my eyes off the sausages on my plate in case some other hungry young devil grabbed them. We had some real characters in those digs, lads who worked at the docks and in the railway works.

I'll never forget my landlady's boyfriend, and she was about sixty-five then, a fellow called Donald. All her life she had worked on the big cruise liners, the *Queen Mary* and the *Queen Elizabeth*. He had worked on the *Mauritania*. He was the biggest fellow I'd ever seen, well over twenty-five stone, absolutely enormous – and a real character. Whenever he was there we'd get him laughing, and he had a real deep-throated roar. The old girl would hear him starting off, she'd come in and think we were all laughing at her. She used to really get mad at us about it.

We used to have some great laughs and it was no exaggeration about having to watch out for the food on your plate. One lad would get your attention for just a couple of seconds, you'd look down and suddenly your sausages and baked potato had disappeared! Stupid antics perhaps, but as kids they were the kind of things you got up to.

If you ever go to a wedding reception or something similar where there's a buffet you can always tell the people who live in digs. They are the ones who get tucked in straight away to the grub, because they know what it's like to have competition. Those days and that education were priceless.

I was dead lucky with my football because I played almost straight away for Southampton reserves – not bad for a kid of fifteen fresh out of the school in the April. Then it was quite rare for someone as young as that to be pitched forward so quickly, whereas these days it happens quite often. I'd had just two or three 'A' team games and there must have been a lot of injuries towards the end of the season, so here I was with my chance in the reserves. It was at Southend, we won 3–2 and I scored the winner. In the team were the likes of Tommy Traynor, an old Saints stalwart, the former

Leicester player Ian White, and David Burnside who had been a young, ball-juggling star at West Bromwich Albion. So we had a fair bit of experience even then.

It was Easter time, just a month away from the end of the season, before I got a bit of time off in the Spring. Apprentices were still fairly new in football at the time and we were required to do odd-jobs around the ground – not that we were ever very good at that. We were too busy larking around. They tried to get us to paint the dressing room one day and I remember one of the lads on the job was a big full-back we had then called Mick Ellard. He had played in that County match for Hampshire against me the day I was spotted by Southampton. I was the one up the ladder and Mick had come in with a lovely, brand new, bright yellow jumper. He was very proud of it, as most kids are with something new.

I'm painting this ceiling and I've got the brush full of paint when suddenly I've flicked it. Poor Mick, this huge dollop of paint has gone right across his yellow jersey. That was the signal for uproar and before long everyone had joined in. We all ended up covered with paint, there was certainly more on us than on the walls and ceiling!

That's the kind of thing that happens when kids get started. I'll always remember Mick and that jumper, he thought he was Jack the Lad in it until I scored that direct hit with the paint.

The next year I was in the reserves nearly all the time until the following Easter Saturday I got in the first team. My first game was versus Bristol City at home and against John Atyeo, the well-known, former England international. I played in three Second Division games that Easter – a sixteen-year-old boy – a year after I'd joined the club. I managed to score on my début along with Terry Paine. John Atyeo got both City's goals in a 2–2 draw.

In those days clubs were definitely run by players – not managers as most of them are now. Ted Bates signed me, was very knowledgeable and an excellent manager, but there was an awful lot of player power. When I was first at The Dell the law was laid down by the likes of Terry Paine, Tony Knapp, who is now the Iceland manager, Jimmy Melia, Campbell Forsyth and John Sydenham.

I remember my first experience of appearing with the senior players. Southampton had two of the hardest men I've ever played against in my life, Cliff Huxford and Dennis Hollywood. I went to go between them in a training session. But their motto was: 'You can go past me; the ball can go past me – but you won't both bloody go past me together!' That was their law – break it, and they'd have your legs off. Those two gave me some terrible kickings, they could really hurt you, but I learned one of the best lessons of my life, to know what's going on and be aware of other people. I also learned to take my knocks without squealing.

There are certain situations where you just can't win, never mind if you're the best player in the world. But you've got to pick those situations out. As a kid you don't know, until you get a right good hiding. You either learn from it or go back and get it again, perhaps badly. Cliff and Dennis hurt me physically, and mentally it made an impression.

Hollywood was the only person I've known who could look you squarely in the eye, tell an absolutely blatant lie – and you'd believe him. 'I won't kick you, you know I wouldn't do that,' he'd say, or 'I didn't do that, you know I didn't'; just when you could feel the bruises coming up. He was the sort who would *wee* on the coals in the sauna. He'd drive you mad and all the time he'd protest his innocence. But you've got to remember the great thing about football is that basically you have a bunch of rascals with little or no education, a cross section of the working class, all pitching in together to help each other out. On the pitch Dennis would kick lumps out of you; off it, he was always immaculate, a very smart Scot who always had a change of clothes in his car. He'd come in looking a bit scruffy, and go out as sharp as a bright, new pin.

In those early apprentice days you had to learn respect –

or the senior players gave you hell. It's different today when the kids back-chat the older pros without thinking twice. Because I'd been in the reserves the seniors probably thought: 'Here's a young lad trying to make his mark,' and they'd look to give me some stick.

One time I went into the first-team dressing room, taking care to knock politely first on the door, and they started slaughtering me over my accent by making country yokel noises. I couldn't help my accent, but I couldn't get out of that dressing room quickly enough.

If I'd gone in that dressing room without bothering to knock it would have been: 'How dare you – who the hell do you think you are?' How times have changed, and I don't think always for the better. These days the apprentices stroll about as if they own the place and if you question them they'll look at you as if you were a piece of dirt. 'You earn your right to be in this first-team dressing room,' those senior pros used to growl at me. I can honestly say I was petrified to go in the first-team dressing room. Unless you had a job to do in there, you just didn't go in.

Southampton had a lovely, old trainer, an ex-Guardsman whose bark was worse than his bite, called Jimmy Gallagher. He was a smashing fellow who'd take us out on the track. In those days you weren't coached. The only instruction you had was playing with your Jimmy Melias, Terry Paines, John Sydenhams and Tony Knapps – good senior players. It would make you laugh today, we'd go on the track and Old Jim would be there looking immaculate with his perfectly groomed moustache and military style. He'd blow a whistle. One burst and you had to start jogging, he blew it again and you stopped. Then another blow and you had to go faster – that was training. Yet it was in the days when we won the World Cup and I'm quite sure that up and down the country at most clubs the training would have been similar. We'd use the car park for five-a-sides, but tactics talks were very rare. All anybody wanted to do was play.

The only problem the young Mick Channon had at that

The Saints' apprentice

time was a player called Martin Chivers, who was already the local hero and an England Under-23 international. I think Ted Bates soon realized that he had two players to fill one position, although he did compromise for a short time by playing me as a left-winger with Chivers and Ron Davies as the spearhead. Little did I know then, as a raw 16-year-old, that in future years I would play alongside Chiv in the full England side.

I always felt that Martin never reached his full potential, although he was a top-class player. Potentially he had everything that you could ever want in a perfect footballer. He was 6ft, quick, good in the air and had a good touch for such a big fellow, but he still lacked that vital, aggressive streak that would have made him an all-time great. I believe that is why Ted Bates let Martin leave Southampton to go to Tottenham for a record fee of £125,000.

It strikes me that apprentices have very little respect for the senior pros these days, but, mind you, a lot of them are playing in the reserves at sixteen today, quite often eight or nine at a time. They are frightened to death of the manager but have no respect for the seniors. It's a bad thing because I don't think you can learn anything from a manager: he can't teach you as much as organize you. He can put things on but if you don't believe in them you're not going to do them. It's sad but that is part of society in general today, you can't get to the kids as much today. The only people that really interest them are those that pay their wages.

In the old days you still had to respect the manager and to go to him about your wages. But there were at least six players at the club as well who would pull you up. However, although I was frightened of those players doesn't mean to say I wasn't as cocky or as confident in my own ability as any of today's youngsters.

2 · Boys on the Black Stuff

Nothing in football gets people more worked up than the selling of Cup Final tickets on the black market. It stirs up the emotions of ordinary fans who can't get a precious ticket and can't afford the black market price. I have every sympathy with the poor punter and I know I'm going to make a lot of people howl in rage when I say I still think it is a justifiable perk for players, most of whom only get one chance in a lifetime to make a few extra bob out of entertaining millions.

I'll tell you, if you go through the members of that Southampton Cup-winning team I can assure you that hardly any of them are living life high off the hog, and quite a few don't even earn the national average. Of course, people squeal at the time, but you can't blame a player wanting to cash in one of the very few assets he is ever likely to have. No one complains about entertainers in show business earning vast fortunes and no one protests about black market prices being charged for big shows. Yet somebody along the line is earning out of it. If demand exceeds supply in any walk of life, you are going to find prices going up.

Let me say straight away, I've sold match tickets to the black market – about half of my allocation went that way for the FA Cup Final in 1976, the rest I gave away to family friends. In later life I've never bothered because I haven't felt I needed the money so badly. When a player is younger he has to be frightened of what lies ahead when he can't kick a ball anymore, so the feeling about building a nest egg can get quite intense.

To ignore the fact that players get perks like this would be to bury your head in the sand as well as being hypocritical. There are plenty of other payments such as money for wearing a certain maker's boots. I can assure you it does go on because I've experienced it myself. But before I am condemned out of hand for my views let me put over a few points.

It's a strange thing that when a team like Southampton is successful, a club which used to average around 14,000 to 15,000 crowds have all of a sudden got 50,000 fans. They are all screaming that they've been regulars for the last ten or twenty years. Friends of friends are suddenly coming out of the woodwork. I disposed of half of my FA Cup Final ticket allocation back in 1976, and gave away the other half, so I certainly didn't make any sort of killing. And I would think that lots of other players have the same kind of story.

Selling tickets on the black market has gone on for years, and the way I look at it is if I come out of it not losing money I am delighted. From talking to players in the game, I know that some clubs actually pay their men *not* to sell their Cup Final tickets in order to keep them out of the hands of touts. I know, and every player knows, that selling tickets to touts has gone on from the earliest days of the game – and that's why I'm not about to sweep it under the carpet and say it doesn't exist. And it doesn't just go on with Cup Finals. When big League games are sell-outs, players have the opportunity to make a few quid with their ticket allocation. One thing I've never done, but I know goes on, is that players also sell their season tickets. Most clubs give their players at least two each. I don't altogether agree with this practice, but having said that I don't begrudge players anything they get.

Before the 1976 FA Cup Final demand for tickets was phenomenal – it always is when you are playing Manchester United, the best supported club in the world. I do know for a fact that tickets that were on sale at our ground were being bought by supporters who were then going outside the gates and making up to £50 profit as the touts snapped them up. There are never any howls of protest at fans making a quick profit. But as soon as a player does something similar, he's out of order and all hell breaks loose. So goodness knows what the fans would have made of one of our star players, Peter Osgood, arriving at Southampton one day with a briefcase stuffed with cash to buy up every ticket he could lay his hands on.

I'll never forget the sight of Ossie, flanked by two of his mates as minders, with £17,000 bulging out of his case. Typically of Ossie, he said: 'Right, there'll be no training this morning until all the tickets are sorted out!' His next order was 'Report to my office.' He'd taken over the players' room to do his business. I thought that he must have been given the cash by one of the big touts to buy up as many tickets as possible – from players and punters – to be sold later on the black market. I'm sure that not all the players did business with Ossie. But the sight of that seventeen grand was something to behold. It was an awful lot of money back in 1976. Ossie did say he was also going to Manchester, so the money might have been to buy tickets up there as well.

I remember one of our players, Jim Steele, took a bit of a chance with his tickets. Apart from your entitlement as a player to buy tickets from the club, you also get given five or six complimentaries – and those you really ought to keep for yourself. That's because you have to sign a form for the complimentaries, saying you won't sell them to anyone above face value. But Jim didn't care, as soon as he got his complimentaries he just shuffled them up with his purchased allocation before getting ready to sell them – the dream of making some easy, ready cash overrode all other considerations.

Even with the allocation of tickets that players bought from the club, they had to give a name and address for where each one was going. That was easily sorted out – a lot of the lads got stuck into the local telephone book putting down any old name and address! There are always loopholes in everything, so that shows you what a complete waste of time it was to have checks on where the tickets were going

Why do players sell tickets like that? Just take a look where the majority of players come from. Footballers, even today, come in the main from the poorer areas of the country. It's not so bad today because just about everybody comes out of a centrally-heated home. In my day as a young player, going back ten or twenty years, the majority of players came from the poor families – we were nearly all Bash Street kids. Most of us had very little education, and when you do get success it's very difficult to know how to handle it. All of a sudden you've got £100 in your pocket when you've been used to having nothing. So when the once-in-a-lifetime chance comes of making some big money out of the FA Cup Final, players tend to take it. This hasn't just started to happen – it's being going on since football first started.

A footballer's life is open to abuse from start to finish. Criticism has never bothered me at all, but it hurts your parents, your wife and kids at school. Now, if that criticism also concerns players earning a bit of extra money when they are offered it, for what is an extremely short-term career, then I think it is unfair. Life isn't all a bed of roses, and unless you can face up to living in the real world where people do sell a few tickets, then you haven't got much hope. If the only crime that some players commit is to sell tickets, it's not such a bad thing.

Certainly there has been no long-lasting bonanza from those days for the likes of Peter Osgood. He's been coaching at holiday camps to try and get himself back on the right road. Footballers are renowned for being bad businessmen and there are always the parasites around who are waiting to take you on and screw you up.

The majority of players are basically decent people, the lad in the street who gets a few quid and gives life a good crack. I wouldn't have wanted to be involved with any other profession half as much. Even now, to me, football is refreshing – it's the truth – real life with no bull involved. We are honest to goodness tradesmen, in the main, topped up with a few craftsmen.

I was touched by a tale I heard last year about a player who had to give away all his medals because he was hard up, FA Cup-winners and League Championship medals, the lot. He sold them all at his door for just £30 – not much for all his treasured mementoes. But those same medals were sold at auction for £1,000 – that's what I call taking advantage of someone. In that light, is selling a few tickets such a bad thing? Where money is involved you'll always have dealers and traders. Human nature being what it is, people will always want to make a few quid – whether it be players or punters – and I don't see a lot of harm in it.

3 · Cashing in on the Cup Final

If I had had my way, Mick Channon wouldn't have been part of that marvellous FA Cup Final triumph over Manchester United in 1976. I had wanted to quit Southampton when I knew we were going to miss out on promotion again. I was fed up with Second Division football and I believed it was affecting my England career. I had been lucky enough to start my career in the First Division and it coincided with Southampton's first-ever spell in the top flight, eight years of it. Although I didn't get my way on a move at that time, I decided to turn in the club captaincy as I thought it hypocritical to be the players' leader when I saw my future elsewhere. So it wasn't me who lifted the FA Cup, surely every small boy's dream.

It was at Christmas 1975 that I went to manager Lawrie McMenemy, asking for a transfer. Peter Rodrigues then became captain and did a very good job, steering us all the way to victory at Wembley. I've always been a great believer that in football the captain must be one of the senior pros who has a strong personality and influence on the club. But I can say quite frankly that it didn't bother me one bit that I wasn't the player to get his hands on the Cup first. Lawrie McMenemy went into print saying that he thought I should have lifted the Cup, but Peter Rodrigues had had a very good career and he deserved his moment of glory. You can't have everyone lifting the thing.

Southampton had some very good players at that time, but

true to form we had some real characters among them. I don't think there's ever been a Southampton team without the boozers and the wild lads who like a good time – and they are no different to me in that sense. Sure they had their shortcomings, but those shortcomings certainly didn't include their attitude to the game – that was first class.

Peter Osgood was near the top of the list as a character. He came to us from Chelsea for £265,000, which was an awful lot of money for Southampton in those days. For me, Ossie during his Chelsea days must rank alongside all the greats I have played with and against. Painey will always be my main man because I was at an impressionable age when I worshipped him, but Ossie was truly a great player.

People talk about Ossie and George Best and moan that they didn't fulfil their careers as they should have done. I do not agree. I believe that Peter Osgood reached his peak between the ages of eighteen and twenty-four. People say he wasted himself because he liked a drink and a good time . . . rubbish. Ossie's approach to training was much better than mine, he'd leave me miles behind, and yet people say he threw everything away. Without that wildness, the likes of Ossie and Best wouldn't have developed their marvellous skills, flamboyance, flair or cheek, call it what you will. I believe those men were right for the very top for five or six years – that's the way it was meant to be.

Perhaps I've been a lucky lad to go all the way through to my late thirties still playing, but they could do things I could never do. All right, they may have had a self-destruct button, but without it they wouldn't have been genuine greats. All geniuses have to be slightly flawed.

I don't regret a single thing in my football career – and I'm sure if you asked Ossie and Best they'd tell you the same. I consider myself fortunate to have played alongside Ossie, although we had some huge rows along the way. But no good player who thinks or cares about the game can go through his career and not have disagreements. Show me one and I'll show you someone who can't play.

Ossie was over the hill when he arrived at Southampton, even though he was hardly into his late twenties. But his enthusiasm and his will to work and play hadn't diminished at all. And it was because of him that we got the FA Cup Final: him and another reject at that time, a lovely Scots lad Jim McCalliog, who, to use a well-worn expression, had more clubs than Jack Nicklaus – a bit like me now!

I'll always remember the free-kick that got us to the semi-final when Ossie flipped the ball up and Jimmy Mac volleyed it into the net against Bradford City. Without that there's a fair chance we wouldn't have got there. You don't lose everything overnight, although I still think it's fair to say we didn't see the best of Peter Osgood at Southampton. But we certainly had some laughs with him. He was a bit like me in that he believed in having a good time. He was still a very capable player but physically he just wasn't up to the training, even if his attitude was still excellent.

One incident summed up Ossie nicely. He'd been up to London for a night out, he'd had a few drinks and his car had gone off the road into a ditch and turned over. He had a purple Capri at that time with the registration PO 9. The next morning in the dressing room there were newspaper pictures of this Capri upside down and some wag had put the letter 'T' into the registration so it read 'PTO' – please turn over! The story goes that the police arrived at the scene and the only reason they knew it was Peter Osgood, as they saw two figures running off across a field, was that the girl was twenty yards in front!

We had another right herbert in that team, a defender called Jim Steele – now he could drink for Scotland, make no mistake about that. In my opinion Jim never quite reached the heights of which he was capable. He messed up his career. He could really play and had limitless potential, but certain aspects of this Scotsman's personality really mucked him up. He wanted to be a big name like Peter Osgood or even Mick Channon, before he'd worked for it. He let himself down at vital moments. But when it came to the crunch in the Cup

Final, for me, he was out on his own as our man of the match.

If Lawrie McMenemy had wanted to, however, he could have kicked out Steeley before his finest hour, along with Ossie and Jimmy McCalliog, who had been the two heroes in the quarter-final. We had just beaten Crystal Palace, Malcolm Allison his fedora and all, 2–0 in the semi-final, and were due to face Portsmouth in an important local derby early the next week. We still had a chance of going up, so Lawrie decided it would be a good thing if we went away to a hotel on Hayling Island to prepare ourselves. But before setting off, he wanted us to turn up at the ground to do a bit of training at six o'clock on the Sunday night. We went in the gym for some stretching exercises and a five-a-side game. Then Lawrie said he wanted everyone in the hotel by nine o'clock that night for a meal. We all turned up, apart from three players – Steeley, Ossie and McCalliog who had all been at the training session. Nothing more was thought of it until later on we learned what had predictably happened. It seemed that a pub had jumped out in the road in front of their car and waylaid them! It was at a place we knew Steeley used quite a lot whenever he made a mooing sound – a famous pub called the Cowherds. Jim Steele had turned up at the hotel to check in, but had rushed away again. It was the next day that we learned they had all been caught by one L.McMenemy as they tried to creep in at around midnight. They were promptly sent home. It was a sensation at the time and thought of as disgraceful behaviour for players who had got to the Final.

We had never known anything like it in Southampton, the whole town had gone mad in anticipation of a trip to Wembley. That's why Lawrie insisted we went in to train on the Sunday night, to get the celebration out of our system in time for the Portsmouth game. As it turned out, Steeley had been trying to be good for once in his life, bless him. He had tried to cover up for the other two and, typically of poor Steeley, had only got himself in more bother. He had gone back out to look for Ossie and Jim only to fall for another drinking session himself – and then it was back into the arms of a very angry Lawrie. Funnily enough, among the three kids that Lawrie threw in to replace the bad lads was Stevie Williams, making his début under strange circumstances. I hate to say that we won 1–0, because I scored. Lawrie's wrath wasn't to last too long and soon after the three lads who had been dropped were back in the side and we were on our way to Wembley. The boys were heavily fined but readily accepted they were in the wrong – they could hardly argue, getting caught red-handed like that.

Steeley came good once in his career, in the 1976 Final. After that he went back into his old ways and let us down at crucial moments. We should have been heading for the European Cup-Winners' Cup semi-final when he went to stop the ball outside the penalty box and let it run under his foot. Van der Elst was there to slap it into the net and Anderlecht ended up beating us 3–2 on aggregate.

So that was the hard core of our Cup Final team. Then we had Rodrigues who had been a good professional and regular for Wales; goalkeeper Ian Turner, whom Lawrie had bought from Grimsby; and centre-half Mel Blyth, who was the tightest man I've ever played with in my life! Mel must have invented meanness where the pocket was concerned.

We had a very good, left-footed lad at left-back, David Peach, who had come from Gillingham – but he's another who has probably still got his first wage packet. I'd swear he used to sew his pockets up on pay day! We did have some tight sods, but I can assure you the others more than made up for it. Paul Gilchrist came in for Hughie Fisher at the last moment, he was a forward who went back into midfield on that occasion, a good player. He was alongside Jim McCalliog, whose reputation definitely went before him!

I remember the day Jim got his driving licence back after a ban, he went out and got a car, celebrated by drinking too much, and ended up crashing it into some traffic lights. I think he'd taken a corner too fast at about four in the

Lawrie's vigil

morning. He walked home and when he got there the police were waiting for him outside the front door.

Steeley was just as crazy, driving about in an old Jaguar. I remember one time when the lads were playing in a darts match and we stayed on for a few pints afterwards. Most of the lads left between half past eleven and midnight and Steeley was the last to go. He lived in a pub anyway so it was no surprise that he lingered longer than the rest. The next morning he came in cut to pieces. He had left the pub, gone straight through a roundabout, turned the Jag over and he had been thrown straight through the windscreen. He had lain in the road with his Jag upside down and people from a nearby house had come out and covered him over with a blanket, thinking he was dead.

Jim Steele was taken to hospital but the police couldn't breathalyse him because he was unconscious. The next day he woke up in hospital, discharged himself and came to the ground! Amazingly there was nothing wrong with him apart from all his cuts and bruises. That was Jim Steele, one wild lad. The last I heard of him he was working in a liquor store in America . . . I couldn't think of anything more appropriate.

All the lads had something to offer or they wouldn't have been where they were. It takes all sorts to make a team. You need your mean man, like Mel Blyth, who would never give anything away; your David Peach who was very careful; your Paul Gilchrist who was very quiet; and your Bobby Stokes who used to work his backside off, apart from getting the winner in the Cup Final. You need all those different men who, if they all knit together, can become a great team.

Southampton had got relegated the year before along with Manchester United, but they went straight back up again. *We* had the same players who had just missed out on going back up, but now they were more experienced. Rodrigues had played in a Cup Final before, as had Ossie and Jim McCalliog, I was a regular international, and we were allied to keen youngsters like Nicky Holmes. We were far more experienced than our opponents, Manchester United.

On the day we knew we could beat United. In my opinion, Lawrie McMenemy was beginning to get the idea of how to manage by then. In that Cup Final season he was just getting to grips with being a boss – I thought 1976 was the year he grew up. He was beginning to know how to handle players and his record since has proved that those days held him in good stead.

I was so lucky because we won the Cup Final on the Saturday and I had my testimonial on the following Monday. It was almost embarrassing for me really because they were queueing for tickets to a testimonial game at six o'clock, Monday morning. Tickets had been on sale for a month anyway and by ten or eleven o'clock on the day they had all gone. Consequently we had season-ticket holders who had missed out in the rush to welcome the FA Cup to The Dell.

It was a great day for Southampton, a club that had never won the Cup before, and here was me cashing in on it. I'll always remember walking into the ground that night and seeing the players of QPR, the opposition, handing their tickets through the coach window to ticket touts. It suddenly hit me just what a big event this was turning into, there were season-ticket holders yelling at me because they hadn't got tickets.

I thought to myself I'm probably the only player who has had tickets to his testimonial sold on the black market!

Financially it couldn't have worked out better at the time. Officially the attendance was 29,000 and the receipts were £23,000. But just imagine if you had 29,000 in the ground today for a testimonial, the receipts would probably be nearer £103,000.

The reason I'd had a testimonial was that I'd been with Southampton since I was a kid. I'd never had a move or any sort of lump sum payment – it was a reward for ten years of loyal service.

Mine was one of the testimonial test-cases, when players were fighting for the payment to be tax free. So it took eight or nine years before that money could be touched. And with inflation being what it was, I can assure you that by the time I got my hands on the cash it was no big total at all. But I was getting paid for doing something that I love so I've got no complaints. It was a very good testimonial, a very good night and the perfect way to celebrate the winning of the FA Cup.

The more success you have, the more you want, and it becomes an obsession. The more people tell you how good you are, the more you believe it, and that was nearly my downfall at Southampton the first time around. There was a period at The Dell when I thought I was above everybody. Saying it now I hate myself. I thought I *was* Southampton and that if Mick Channon left, the club would fold up. Part of that is immaturity, part of it is being over-confident and having an enormous ego. It was brought home to me at my peak in 1976 by the most unlikely person, Peter Osgood, that happy-go-lucky extrovert who gave the appearance of strolling through life with a smile on his face. But he was deadly serious when he suddenly turned on me.

Sometimes we used to train at Hampshire's county cricket ground in Southampton as they had a grassy car park that served as a good five-a-side pitch. Lawrie McMenemy had barely been at Southampton a couple of years so he wasn't such an influential figure at that stage. I remember going in one morning feeling out of sorts, not wanting to train. Whether I'd had a bad night or got out of bed the wrong side I don't know, but I'll never forget Ossie rounding on me. I was hardly bothered and probably messing up the training. I thought I was bigger and more important than anyone. Ossie snapped: 'I've come all the way from Windsor to train – if you don't want to bother yourself, push off!'

For Ossie to turn on somebody at that time was most unusual as he had his own problems, he had found it difficult to settle into the team and he'd been in and out. But he'd come all the way from Windsor every day, an hour's drive on the motorway, and he wanted to train hard. I hadn't wanted to know and I must have been a right pain in the backside. After that morning it didn't sink in right away, but I suddenly said to myself: 'Who do you think you are?' Ossie had been dead right. I had thought I was bigger than the club and that annoyed me. It's something that happens with footballers occasionally and I like to think that from then on, although I've never been the best trainer, I didn't mess up anybody else's efforts at trying to enjoy their training.

Some players, like Ossie, have to work very hard to get the best out of their training, whereas I was fortunate that I didn't have to work too hard to keep in good shape. At that time poor old Ossie was fighting for his life to stay in the game while I still had plenty of years left. He used to work at it and I probably didn't – I owed him more than that. It was a good bit of shock treatment that made me realize how selfish it was to have too big an ego, to think I was better than anyone else. But I also realized that it was time to move on from Southampton, I had been there too long. I needed another challenge. I had got the feeling that I was indispensable. I feel it happens today at certain clubs, particularly West Ham where they never seem to let players go. They can get casual and lackadaisical, and not fired up enough to win things. The same could be said, to a certain extent, of rural clubs like Ipswich and even Southampton. Because they always keep close-knit families and never get rid of anyone they probably loose the killer instinct of a winner.

4 · The Ale House Lads

The late, great Liverpool manager, Bill Shankly, came out with one of football's classic quotes back in the 1960s when he called Southampton 'Ale House brawlers' after we'd beaten Liverpool 1–0 at The Dell. Poor old Bill didn't realize just how near to the truth he was. To give you an indication of what I mean, I'll go back to an incident long before that smashing victory of ours over one of England's best club sides in modern times.

Ted Bates was the manager and John Mortimore, now boss of Portugal's top club Benifica, was the No. 2. We'd played at Sunderland and lost 1–0 on the Saturday before going on for a midweek game at Burnley. Ted Bates had to go back South, so Mortimore was in charge. We stayed up in Harrogate, Yorks, to prepare for the game. I was only a kid, barely eighteen, not long in the team, and playing up front with Ron Davies. There were other great characters in the team at that time like Jimmy Melia, Terry Paine, John Sydenham, Brian O'Neil, Hughie Fisher, Jimmy Gabriel, John McGrath and Dennis Hollywood.

We'd sat down for a meal at our hotel, Mortimore had come in and, not having been at Saints long, tried to make an impression. He said: 'Right lads, everyone in bed by eleven o'clock tonight – curfew.' All the lads looked at each other, thinking: 'What the hell's going on here? We're not playing till the Tuesday.' So the word went round – one out, all out.

There had never been any discipline at Southampton ever before, but old Ted Bates knew how to handle people. John Mortimore, a new fellow, a new face, wanted to make an impression – but he soon realized it was the wrong one with lads like us. Ted Bates would say to us: 'You can go and have a drink, but don't fill your boots.' All Mortimore had done was to put down a challenge that the lads gladly took up!

It was about one o'clock in the morning and we were still out in a club in Harrogate. I'd had plenty to drink for a young lad and was looking to go home. Jimmy Melia by this time was well out of the game, out of his famous bald head with drink (the head that was later to become so famous when Jim was manager of Second Division Brighton in the 1983 FA Cup Final against Manchester United).

Poor old Jimmy, he was a pretty sensible fellow who looked after himself and I'll always remember before he went out on that Harrogate night he said to me: 'Don't go over the top, Mike, you're a young lad.' And I said: 'Don't worry, Jim.' It was an old pro, Jim, looking after a young pro, me. By about midnight in this club, Jim's in a corner and the lads are having little snacks in baskets like scampi and chips. He was much the worse for wear and slumped in his seat, and the boys have perched one of these food baskets on his bald head. It was an uproarious sight with the boys all helping themselves to chips from Jim's head basket while he didn't know a thing about it!

Ron Davies and I decided to take Jim home at this stage so we called a cab and just about carried him to it. But when we arrived back at the hotel, after one in the morning, there were John Mortimore and trainer George Horsfall in reception – and there was no way past them without being discovered. We went looking for a back entrance with no luck. There was only one thing for it and we propelled Jimmy through the revolving doors. You've never seen a sight like it as Jimmy Melia went tottering out the other side – now I know where he got his reputation for disco dancing, with those famous white shoes so well publicized when he managed Brighton to Wembley!

Jimmy staggered across the foyer and up to bed. We could see trainer George Horsfall was there to tick off the names of people on a list as they came through, so Ron and I dutifully went on in.

There was a big meeting called for the next morning and John Mortimore tried to give us a rollicking – but if there was one thing John was never very good at, it was bawling people out, because you could never take him seriously. He was trying to make an impression but with the lads we had there, nothing washed. I was only a youngster then and I'll always remember the old hands laughing themselves silly at my fumbled attempts to make an excuse on everyone's behalf. But then I realized that they had been out on the town as well so I just got more and more tongue-tied – the meeting ended in uproar. That was poor John's initiation to Southampton and from then on he could never really succeed with the older lads who more or less lost respect for him there and then.

It was big John McGrath, our centre-half, who got us nicknamed the Ale House team by Shanks. It was after that 1–0 win over the Reds, the goal coming from yours truly. John was a massive bloke and had got involved with Liverpool's striker, Alun Evans. Alun had gone to head the ball and John's nut crashed into the back of his head, knocking him out. It looked very serious at the time; Alun had swallowed his tongue. But defenders smacking you in the back of the head happens all the time. I'm still getting plenty of that up to this very day.

On another occasion at Chelsea when big John came up against Ian Hutchinson, one of the bravest centre-forwards around, I remember one of the funniest newspaper reports I've ever read on a football match. It was by Peter Batt in *The Sun* and he wrote something like this: John McGrath went into a tackle with Ian Hutchinson and they both fell to the ground. McGrath rose to his feet and gingerly tested his

Big Bad John

giant legs. But he shouldn't have worried – because nothing less than a pneumatic drill could have harmed them.' That assessment of the rugged John McGrath was spot-on.

Then there was Jimmy Gabriel, an amazing character who used to play at the back alongside McGrath. Jimmy had been a big star at Everton when they were a great team, and he was still a more than useful player with us. If you went by him in training he'd say: 'Don't do that again son.' If you did, more than likely he'd give you a good kick. In those days there was no friendship if it was club mate against club mate on the training pitch. All right, people say they weren't good professionals in those days at Southampton because they used to drink and have a good time. But I tell you what, their attitude to competition was first class. You had to be smart, even in training, if you wanted to learn how to avoid a battering. You were taught good habits. The professional approach of those lads towards playing was second to none, even though everything else in life was there to be enjoyed.

You don't get mongrels in the jungle, but you do at a football club. They come from everywhere and from all backgrounds, they're like crossbreds when they all get together.

Jim Gabriel was a real Scotsman – proud, passionate, everything that I love about a footballer – a stubborn devil and I hated him at times. But you'd never ever question his professionalism or his dedication. He loved his football and had that enthusiasm that used to drive him mad when he thought he hadn't played well – that was Jimmy. He wanted to be the best. And the only Englishman I know who was as intense as that about the game, apart from me, was Alan Ball. There are hundreds of Scotsmen who have got it, that's probably why I've got it in for them so much north of the Border!

The Southampton players would have a good Saturday night like teams all over the country, then it would be Sunday lunch-time down the Gateway, a local pub. We'd get in there for twelve o'clock and set the world to rights. Things are never as bad the next day. Whatever happens – if you've won, its better . . . if you've got beat, it's not quite so bad, especially with a few pints inside you.

Jim was getting on a bit then, and one Sunday he said: 'Right, it's time I started watching my weight. After today, I'm not going to touch another drop.'

We had a right good Sunday lunch-time drink and staggered home to our dinner. Next morning Jim came in to training, proclaiming quite proudly that he hadn't had another drink. He had a slight hangover from the previous lunch-time, but no alcohol had passed his lips on Sunday night. Then it started, no drinks on Monday night, Tuesday, Wednesday or Thursday. Finally he came in on Friday morning absolutely stinking of booze – you couldn't get within ten yards of him for smelling the stuff.

I remember the lads saying to him: 'I thought you were on the wagon for a month.' 'You won't believe this,' he told us, 'but I was sitting on the sofa in front of the television last night, the missus had gone to bed, and I was watching "High Chaparral". A cowboy has come in the bar and ordered up a bottle of whisky. It was slid down the bar to him, he put it to his lips and gargled it all back, almost in one action.

'I just couldn't believe that was possible. So I got up, went to the cabinet, got a bottle of Scotch – and I drank it! I just wanted to see if it could be done. At the end of it I couldn't get out of the chair I was so legless. I had to throw a shoe up at the ceiling to get the wife down and help me to bed. She had to drag me up the stairs.'

That was the man – but he would never ever let you down come Saturday. He'd roll up his sleeves and he'd be prepared to die for you. But there was an artistic side, would you believe, to Jimmy. That other great little Scottish character from those Southampton days, Hughie Fisher, tells of the time he was invited into the Gabriel household for a drink. Suddenly Jimmy got out these poetry books and started reciting. Hughie couldn't believe what he was hearing. It wasn't really his scene – he just had to get out, double quick!

I always laugh when I think of the antics of our midfield terror from that era, Brian O'Neil. He's still a drinking mate of mine to this day, although he's long since been out of the game.

Southampton had a gym with an asbestos roof and John Mortimore used to worry about the ball damaging it during training. So he tried to get us to keep the ball below head height in the five-a-sides. The lads weren't having that, in the gym it was every man for himself and there used to be some right battles. We couldn't be worrying about keeping the ball down.

Brian was a real tough nut and all hell used to be let loose where he was concerned. He suddenly larrupped a shot that smashed into the roof – and a big tile came crashing down. Morty gave him a real rollicking, and that gave rise to the most marvellous caricature of the incident by our great centre-forward Ron Davies, who had great talent as a cartoonist. Mortimore was a cartoonist's dream, with his rather large nose, and Ron's drawing had little Brian underneath, booting the ball up his nostrils!

Brian was the only professional player I have known who never had his own pair of football boots – he'd always be on the scrounge for someone else's. He'd use anybody's he could get hold of – and we're talking about a top class player who had appeared for England Under-23s, while he was at Burnley, and for the Football League. He was on the fringe of being a full international – goodness knows what Sir Alf Ramsey would have made of a player who didn't even own the footwear that gave him a living.

Whatever was left in the boot room, Brian would nick for any particular game. I'd seen him in the boot room on match days, rummaging about for a pair and saying: 'They're not bad!' Fridays before away games were a nightmare for our trainer George Horsfall who'd say: 'Brian, what boots are you using this week?' Poor George would make sure the other first-team boots were packed before Brian could get his hands on a pair he fancied.

Brian probably did have a pair of boots from the club originally, but once they'd worn out he obviously never bothered to get the club to replace them. Yet that, for me, shows a great attitude towards the game – there were no excuses like you get these days about the length of your studs not being quite right for a particular surface. If the length of your stud is the difference between playing badly and playing well, then I've been wasting my time all these years. Brian showed it didn't matter a hoot – so long as you had the ability to play.

Brian was so straightforward. We'd come in at half-time in a game when things were going badly and manager Ted Bates would try and lift us. Terry Paine would say something. I'd be having a go and maybe Ron Davies would be having his two pennyworth. Then suddenly Brian would stand up and shout: 'To hell with it, let's get our sleeves rolled up and steam into these buggers.' In other words, hang everything else, let's get straight out there and have a right good crack. We still got beat many a time, but teams had at least felt our steel, thanks to Brian's gee-ups.

The midfielder was as hard as they come. He'd tackle you from any angle, never mind from behind, but he wouldn't go over the top to you. Still, you knew you were going to get it. He'd go for the ball, but too bad if your legs were in the way. He was tackling the ball, basically, and in those days there was nothing to stop the challenge from behind.

A classic case of Brian's hardness came against Spurs. I recall we were playing one of Ted Bates's systems, 1–9–1, with just me left to forage up front on my own. I think Ron Davies must have been out injured. The ball was knocked up to me and Mike England, who has been the Welsh team manager in recent years, gave me such a clattering it makes me grimace to think of it even today. Afterwards he explained to me that he had to kick me because the ball was there. My leg being in the way had made no difference.

I was left on the ground, writhing in agony, the team's goalscoring lifeline and the lads' one chance of getting a few quid from a win bonus. Everyone else was dogging and scrapping for all they were worth. Those were hard days for little Southampton, fresh to a mighty First Division packed with great teams – Manchester United with Best, Law and Charlton; Leeds with the likes of Bremner, Giles and Jones; Liverpool and their Yeats, St John and Smith. Even Sunderland had people like Baxter and Herd. And Tottenham with our old player Martin Chivers, plus Jimmy Greaves and Dave Mackay, were no pushovers either.

There I was in so much pain with the referee telling me to hurry up when Brian O'Neil came thundering over and snapped: 'What number was that?' He wasn't worried who it was, or even if I was all right. He just wanted a number so he could take retribution in his very own way, and to hell with reputations. That one sentence suddenly made me feel like a million dollars, the hurt was gone. It was the kind of camaraderie that I feel has gone out of the game a bit today. You were all together, no matter how good or bad you were. And that's why rugby is such a good game, everyone seems to be together. Whereas in our game there's possibly too much of every man for himself.

Brian's a labourer who sub-contracts these days. He'll dig ditches, holes in the roads, footings . . . anything. But he is *exactly* the same guy and plays in the odd charity game. He's always around for a drink and I know which local to find him in most Sundays.

Brian's great drink in the old days was vodka and water, 'vodka agua' he used to say whenever we were abroad, and he could really lash it down. Never more so than on one trip to Japan, after we'd played a tour game in Kobe. Suddenly our right-back, Ken Jones, who had a history of bad luck hitting him, said to Brian in a bar: 'You can't drink.' Brian told Ken not to be silly because he'd get murdered in that kind of contest. So there was a drinking challenge, the kind that happens a million times between sportsmen when they are relaxing after an event, particularly in rugby circles.

The two of them went at it, drink for drink all night, beers and vodkas. They were stood at the bar while the rest of us were playing darts. At about one in the morning Ken, a good Yorkshireman who certainly could put it away, swallowed the last dregs of yet another drink, while Brian had half a glass left. The next second, Brian's drink has gone but all of a sudden the floor beneath him was soaking wet. Ken went mad, shouting at Brian accusingly: 'You threw that on the floor.' So there was a row and all the lads gathered round.

Terry Paine, laughing himself silly, then sniggered: 'No he hasn't – Brian's pissed himself.' Certainly Brian's grey trousers had turned a very dark colour and all of the lads were falling about, doubled up with laughter. Cocky little Painey loved to take the micky out of everyone and this was even better for him because Brian was his room mate. But you should have seen his face when I turned round and announced; 'By the way lads, Brian put Painey's trousers on to come out tonight!' That was one time when the always immaculate Terry Paine was undone by that habit Brian had of borrowing things – this time it had spread from boots to trousers!

We may have been a bit of a rag-bag outfit but we were still good enough to qualify for Europe, in the old Fairs Cup back in 1969–70. It was Southampton's first competitive trip into Europe and we pulled a Portuguese team called Guimaraes, a two-and-a-half-hour coach trip south of Oporto. This first trip to the unknown was an exciting time and sure enough we were out to enjoy it. A few drinks were taken on the plane out there. The Press joined in, and let's just say that the hospitality was great! We stayed overnight in Oporto before the coach trip to Guimaraes. It was red hot weather and we roasted all the way. When we got there we found a brand new stadium that wasn't quite finished. In the dressing rooms there were bare brick walls and simple chairs. There were no showers and not even any running water. We just got on with it and ended up with a very creditable 4–4 draw, after leading 4–2. Throats were burning after all this effort but with no running water it looked as though we would have to suffer and sweat all the way back to Oporto.

Before the game had started, the Guimaraes team had come out and presented every one of our players with a vintage bottle of port, the whole squad of sixteen. Yet afterwards there hadn't even been a bottle of Coke to quench our raving thirsts. There was just one thing for it, the only drinking liquid available was the vintage port. We didn't need to fly in a plane that day because by the time we got back to Oporto every bottle of port had been drunk dry.

Players, management, directors and Press, we were all in together on that coach to the airport. And by the time we got on the plane just about everyone was pickled. Bawdy songs, cruel jokes aimed at parts of the anatomy, like coach John Mortimore's nose, it had been another great time out for the Ale House lads. But we ended up beating the Portuguese in the home leg and going on in the competition, only getting knocked out on the away-goals rule by Newcastle in the last sixteen.

One of the lovely things about being part of that Southampton team was being managed by Ted Bates. He was a caring human being who understood the weaknesses in his fellow man. The qualities were perfectly illustrated on a pre-season tour to West Germany. Football was different then and it wasn't so disciplined. Ted had sent us all to the pictures one afternoon, but that wasn't much good to a bunch of lads who couldn't understand a word of German between them. There was only one alternative for the Ale House lads, the nearest bar we could find. It may have been the day before a game, but it didn't matter to our team. To us there was no harm in having a pint or three the day before a game. Little did we know that Ted Bates was taking out the chairman and the Southampton *Evening Echo* journalist, Brian Hayward, along with John Mortimore and George Horsfall, the trainer.

Ted decided to take them for a drink and he was about to walk into the bar where all the boys were having their beer.

He looked round the corner, spotted us and promptly turned on his heel before the chairman could walk in the door and see us, saying: 'This is too rough a place for us, we'll go to a different pub.' He was discreet enough to know that the chairman wouldn't appreciate seeing us out on the town. But he also knew that at the end of the day he wouldn't be let down by the team. Some managers would have gone berserk and read the riot act. Not Ted, he knew what we were and planned accordingly.

Don't forget I'm talking about a group of footballers who were basically a bunch of scallywags and such things happen when such characters get together. But I have no hesitation in saying that I was proud to be a junior member of the Ale House lads. Despite the champagne life that was to come later on with England, becoming the highest-paid player in the country with Manchester City and then my times back at The Dell with Kevin Keegan and Alan Ball, nothing could have been sweeter than those marvellous early years.

5 · What a Paine

I have no hesitation in naming Southampton's Terry Paine as the greatest player I've played with. But having said that, he was an aggressive character who could be a right Paine in the neck. I've played with some greats like Bobby Moore, Alan Ball and Kevin Keegan. And I've faced Franz Beckenbauer and Johann Cruyff and George Best. But Terry Paine comes out on top of the heap for me.

I'd say that 60 to 70 per cent of my knowledge of the game has come from Terry Paine; or from Ted Bates, my first manager. It certainly didn't happen overnight. He used to say things to me and try to get me to do things. But it wasn't until I was on the same wavelength that I realised how much he meant to me. In the end Terry Paine only had to look at me. I've scored hundreds of goals for Southampton just by catching a glance from Painey. As soon as our eyes met – I know it sounds a stupid thing to say – I knew what he was going to do. I knew he was going to knock that ball over from the wing. He and I knew – but the defender marking me didn't know so I could steal a vital yard on him so many times.

Terry was only a slight fellow but he could beat anyone, and he was a great crosser of the ball. In my early days he was still a top man for England and, of course, was in the World Cup-winning squad of 1966.

Painey, however, was hated by nearly everyone in the game at one stage or another. He had a great knack of getting up everyone's nose. He had a terrible reputation for going over the top in the tackle and kicking people. But, I tell you what, he could play. Having that rotten streak in him made him the player and competitor he was. He would kick his own mother and could be really nasty. He wasn't the bravest of players, he wouldn't go up face to face and kick you. But he would take every advantage. Not many people took liberties with him and everybody wanted to kick him. He wasn't much different from Johnny Giles and probably liked about as much. Loads of people thought bad thoughts of Gilesy and wanted to top him. Players like that normally build up a long list of people wanting to go on revenge missions, but Painey was too shrewd to get done.

Ted Bates always said that the mark of a good player is the number of years he plays after reaching the age of thirty. Terry went on to his late thirties, had eighteen years with Southampton and a club record of 713 League games. He really was Mr Southampton. He took some criticism about being Ted Bates's blue-eyed boy but he deserved to be called Mr Southampton because he made them tick.

In later years I took over that mantle to a certain degree. As soon as Lawrie McMenemy arrived as prospective manager he clashed with Painey, perhaps because he knew the little man was so well loved. As it turned out Terry lasted only another year.

Lawrie's pet hate was the title that Southampton gave him at first: Manager Designate, as he was put on something of a trial period to prepare for Ted Bates's retirement. That tag used to get right up his nose – along with Painey's amazing popularity. It was no coincidence that Terry was ousted so quickly. They simply couldn't stand each other. They both had dominating personalities and both wanted to be top man. A similar situation arose much later between Lawrie and Kevin Keegan. They were two very strong people. I'm a strong character as well and I was in among that situation, but I never wanted to run the club.

McMenemy knew that Painey was Mr Southampton and

Contracts out on Terry

if he wanted that title he'd have to get rid of him. The first year McMenemy was at the club we had twenty-five points and were fifth top in the First Division by Christmas. Lawrie was given the manager's job, after stories leaked out around the club that he'd been offered the boss's post at Nottingham Forest. We ended up getting relegated that season. Without doubt there was a certain amount of rebelling against him, and I think that even Lawrie would admit he wanted to change things too quickly. Painey had been in the team all the time until Christmas, then Lawrie left him out and the writing was on the wall for Terry.

To be fair to McMenemy the slide had started before he dropped Painey. But you could feel the tension at that time between the two and this scent of rebellion from the senior players was in the air. I disagreed with a lot of what McMenemy did at the time. His knowledge of football was then limited. He was more involved with the power struggle, about becoming 'The Boss'. He wanted to change the coach and get rid of Ted Bates's influence so that he could rule unhindered. He had so much on and wanted to do a great deal in very little time therefore he made a right balls up of it.

Painey must have wondered what would have happened if he'd still been around. We certainly missed his great talents although, to do justice to McMenemy, Terry wasn't getting any younger.

At his best Terry had great pace over ten yards and could beat four or five opponents straight off with his trickery rather than his running. He was a jinker rather than a runner, and a great crosser of the ball. Certainly Ron Davies wouldn't have scored half the goals he did without Paine. He was brilliant at getting to the byline, and cutting that ball back. It was perfect for big Ron, who stands out as the best header of a ball I've ever seen, let alone played with or against. Ron wasn't just accurate with his headers, he used to rifle that ball in. He should have been born with a boot on his head.

Painey loved to infuriate those big full-backs who yearned

to give him a good kicking. He made them look daft. As for gamesmanship, Terry could have invented the concept.

I was a stubborn, cocky, little so-and-so in my early years at Southampton. I was in my late teens when I had a fight with Terry Paine. I was playing in the first team and we had a disagreement. As I've said, Terry had a great talent for getting under people's skin, he'd keep niggling away at you and in the end you'd lose your rag. I flew at him, pushed him over and we had a bit of a scrap. But generally, things began to fall into place for me and I began to understand him more. It was then that I realized what a great man he was.

Older players like him used to drive me mad when I was a kid at the club. Often I wondered what they were talking about. I had my disagreements with Painey because I couldn't understand the man earlier on. Now I am sometimes aware of frustrations the younger players have with me. I do understand them because I went through it. It takes you ages to get it all together as a player. When it comes together, it's easy – that's why I'm still playing at thirty-seven. But I owe so much to Terry Paine, I couldn't have had better teaching from anyone.

6 · Nightmare at Maine Road

I call my two years at Manchester City the most traumatic period of my life, never mind my career. We had won the FA Cup in 1976 at Southampton and I had another season there before I was finally on my way. We had done really well in the last year – getting to the quarter-final of the European Cup-Winners' Cup – but we still hadn't got out of the Second Division. I had decided that I had to go and had a fair bit of wrangling with Lawrie McMenemy. By this time he was beginning to become Mr Southampton and he was pretty secure in his own career.

I thought, if I'm going to make the break I must do it now. I was twenty-eight and I knew Manchester City were keen from some interesting conversations I'd had on England's summer tour in South America. The City chairman, Peter Swales, was an FA Councillor and I remember speaking to him in our hotel in Brazil. He made it pretty plain to me that City would be more than interested if I ever thought about a move. And at that time it was common knowledge that if Peter Swales wanted somebody – he got him. By this time I knew I had a pretty good chance of leaving anyway so Swales wasn't doing anything out of order, it was just one of those friendly conversations. He wasn't trying to steal me away.

After a bit more haggling with the board and Lawrie it was decided I could go. The transfer fee was £300,000. So I got the phone call to go and meet Tony Book, the City manager, at the usual sort of rendezvous for these things, just off a motorway. Then I was taken up to chairman Swales's lovely house in Altrincham where I also met another director, Mr Humphreys, from the sports goods company Umbro.

As well as City's interest, I also got an offer from a top French club, Bordeaux, to join them. Three days before I went up to see Peter Swales I met an agent, the same guy who sorted out Kevin Keegan's transfer from Liverpool to Hamburg. I saw him at the Post House Hotel, Heathrow and he talked in terms of a £60,000 signing on fee for me plus around £50,000 a year basic – again pretty big money even now, let alone the mid 1970s. But the agent wanted 10 per cent of everything that I earned. It was a very good offer and with a bigger lump sum up front, probably even better than City's fantastic deal. But it meant leaving the country, learning a different language and at twenty-eight I didn't particularly want to go abroad. Knowing the City was in the pipeline and that they'd finished runners-up in the First Division the year before, I also thought that it was simply a case of going to Maine Road and winning the championship. That was something I'd always wanted to do. So I plumped to stay in England and although my championship dreams went sadly wrong, I don't regret a single minute of it.

Surprisingly, I was quite nervous that day at Peter Swales's house, even though by this time I was an established England international who had seen a lot of the world. Remember I had been a very highly paid player at Southampton – yet I sat there as they started talking terms, and I didn't have to open my mouth. The deal I was offered absolutely staggered me. There was money put into pension funds for me and there's no doubt that the move to City secured my future. Even if I can't say I'll never have to work again, I certainly wouldn't have to draw the dole.

For a three-year contract I had £46,000 for starters going into a pension fund, and that was before I'd drawn a penny in wages. The bonuses themselves were unbelievable, well over £100 a point. Playing for a top team like City – you were almost guaranteed to get sixty points in a season – it meant an awful lot of money, especially in the late 1970s.

It was money for jam – no wonder Manchester City got into such terrible financial problems that they are still getting over them to this very day. It was all caused by the chairman's passionate desire to have a club greater than Manchester United. They had a gigantic chip on their shoulder. A very laudable ambition it may have been, but the way they went about trying to go one better than United was suicidal. I've got an awful lot of respect for Peter Swales because I know he is a very genuine fellow who dearly wants Manchester City to be the best club in the country. I know he has had his critics and people accused him of being a dictator at Maine Road, but I couldn't help admiring his quest to be the best. If that's wrong then there's an awful lot of people who've got different ideas to me.

City were a great club when I was there, nothing was too much trouble. The whole staff were tremendous from the secretary right down to the groundsman. The only problem I had was on the pitch.

There's no doubt in my mind I was the highest paid player in the country, even when I was at Southampton – so the City deal just put me way out on my own. But my playing form wasn't worth two bob. That £300,000 fee was a British record for a few days, until Liverpool signed Kenny Dalglish.

The first strange thing that struck me in that initial meeting at Peter Swales's house was that the manager Tony Book hadn't said a word. It wasn't long before it became apparent to me that Tony Book was greatly influenced by Peter Swales. And he still is to this very day.

I'm not saying that Tony Book isn't a hard worker, but he can't relate to people in general or, even more importantly as a manager, to players in particular. Consequently he could never be consistently successful at the highest level. In saying that I know City won the Milk Cup when he was manager, but you look at the players there at that time: Joe Corrigan,

Willie Donachie, Mick Doyle, Asa Hartford, Peter Barnes, Dennis Tueart, Dave Watson and Joe Royle, internationals all. He couldn't get a team that really gelled out of those players. I don't blame the players. Good players make good teams, but a manager has got to be able to put them together. If Asa Hartford or I weren't right for the job, then we should have been got rid of by the manager. Players must be blended together so they all have respect for one another. It is not enough to be a bunch of talented individuals, which we turned out to be.

There was a tremendous power struggle among the players as to who was in charge. Was it Dennis Tueart, Joe Royle, Asa Hartford, Peter Barnes or Mick Channon? And because the manager wasn't very positive or an especially good leader the struggle to be top man came on the pitch. So then you had people pulling in different directions.

Tony Book's assistant was Bill Taylor, the England coach who died so tragically of a brain tumour. Bill was very honest, a hard worker who believed a lot in theory. He did nothing wrong.

Book's lack of control as a manager was perfectly illustrated on a pre-season tour, after my first bad term at Maine Road. We had qualified for Europe so it wasn't all doom and gloom. With the class of player we had, we were still reasonably successful. Booky never had the personality or the warmth, I thought, to gain the respect of the people who worked for him. He got on really well with our goalkeeper Joe Corrigan. A lot of the lads used to think Joe was a bit too friendly with the boss. Joe certainly stuck up for Book a great deal, along with Paul Power – but they were the team's Mancunians.

Manchester City went on tour to Norway, playing five or six games as a warm-up to the forthcoming season. We'd played one night in Frederikstad and after the game Booky set an eleven o'clock curfew. I've always found curfews very childish, from the days when I was a junior member of the Ale House gang! They wouldn't stand for it, and I saw no reason to start now. I'd much rather a manager had a quiet word in my ear and just asked me to be sensible. It's my life – not yours or anybody else's. I hold that precious. I want to do what I want to do and if I want to go out for a couple of drinks at twenty-nine years of age no one in this world is going to say: 'No Micky Channon, you can't because you're going to get drunk.'

The team had trained hard, played a game and we deserved a bit of relaxation and a few drinks if necessary. Only two of us broke the curfew – Asa Hartford and me. It was strange how we got caught. We were at a night club. I was having a dance on the floor and I swung right round into . . . Tony Book! It was all innocent fun with Bill Taylor and Booky sitting there having a beer. But it led to probably the biggest confrontation I've ever had in my life.

The following day Bill Taylor called a team meeting at the hotel. We all piled in, with Asa and yours truly knowing we were in trouble. It was my intention to say nothing. We had been caught red handed. What could we say? Get your wrist slapped and get on with it, was the way I saw it.

Bill Taylor started: 'About last night . . .' I jumped in: 'Just a minute, with all due respect, you can't have a meeting about people breaking the curfew without the manager being here. So you either get the manager – or the meeting's off.' The whole room went quiet. Off trooped Bill and ten minutes later he came back with Tony. Booky sat down and then went on about having been the manager for three or four years. He had his grumpy, solemn face on. Then he said something like: 'If that's all the respect I get from the players then I'm going to resign.' I immediately responded: 'That will do me!' As I said that the whole room erupted. Joe Corrigan shouted: 'Hold on, let's have a bit of sense here,' because it had become a head-to-head between Tony Book and Mick Channon. Everyone was trying to get a bit of sanity back into the meeting.

Once everything settled down Bill Taylor, bless his memory, said: 'Let's get this straight – in the beginning of the season, you sign a contract, right?' Everyone nodded.

'And if you sign a contract you belong to Manchester City for twenty-four hours a day.' I just saw red and bellowed: 'You what? Nobody owns me!' That was it, all hell was let loose again. Asa Hartford thought the other lads were blaming us because from then on there was a curfew every night. I remember Asa saying: 'You miserable devils.' It was getting to be us against them. However, that was the beginning of the end for Booky.

After that row I felt a power I had never had before in my career. Management were frightened of me. After that they would never, ever take me on again – verbally. They might want to smash me or kick me, but face to face Tony Book and Bill Taylor would never prevail in an argument with me. Indeed, they never did take me on again. Keep out of his way, anything for a quiet life – that was the way I thought they felt towards me. It was a strange feeling; they didn't want confrontation with me. They had had it once and they didn't like what they got.

My biggest problem was on the field itself. I only seemed to get a touch of the ball when everybody else had finished with it. And because I was quick and needed the ball early, it was no good. Forwards need time to create something, so the earlier I got the ball, the better. Say in one second you can run ten yards, half a second five and so on, in a sixteenth of a second you can run half a yard. What do you need to score goals? A split second. So if you can get the ball a second earlier you've probably got five to ten yards to work in. So one hundredth of a second is probably the equivalent of an inch, which may be a case of getting your toe there and scoring a goal before someone else can get to you. That's how important time can be and it didn't suit me the way we were playing. It wasn't a flowing type of game. It wasn't the game I was used to – I couldn't adjust that quickly.

Then there was the conflict of wills going on. Dennis Tueart wanted the game played differently to suit him because he was a wide player. Peter Barnes wanted a similar style and when he got the ball he wanted to take the lace out of it. I was never getting a kick and when I got it I had to turn myself inside out to have any chance. When I did get it I tried to do my own thing and that's how it went on. It was a knock-on effect. You had Joe Royle who was one of the best headers of a ball in the game trying to fit in with two wingers who wanted to just run with it and score goals themselves. I felt that Tony Book just could not handle the situation.

Not long after I had arrived at City I got the worst injury of my career, a pelvic strain that kept me out some six weeks. I was lucky because that problem has finished a lot of people. After that set-back football became a nightmare for me. If I hadn't been such a stubborn, single-minded lad and not believed in myself in the way I did, I could have been kicked all over the place. I was given some nasty treatment, and plenty of verbal abuse. There were chants of: 'What a waste of money' when I'd only been there six or seven months. I thought to myself: either I curl up and die or dig in and go for gold. I dug in and I'm quite sure it was Manchester City that made me grow up as a person. Footballing-wise I didn't have a very good time, but as a man I'd had to fight the world. They were the two black years of my career, but I came through them.

Funnily enough, the situation turned for me when Malcolm Allison arrived. Perhaps I was starting to get my own way and have that little bit of freedom – it was a new start under Malcolm, a new challenge. In the early days he picked me and believed in me. To say I responded was an understatement – I scored eleven goals in thirteen games for him.

It came as no shock when Booky was relieved of his duties, but it was a weird situation because he didn't leave the club. Book became a sort of general manager with Malcolm Allison running the show. We all knew that Malcolm picked the team and we played it Malcolm's way.

The film *One Flew over the Cuckoo's Nest* could have been made for Malcolm. He was away on his own planet. He'd say let's play with no centre-forward and two wingers. At

The square peg

free-kicks he wanted a defensive wall *and* someone standing on the post in case of a curling shot, even though the keeper should have had a proper sight and been able to deal with those. I believe Luton tried that out last season, so it's obviously made a mark on someone – we all thought it was a crazy situation.

From February through to the end of the season I probably played as well as I had done at any time for City. But it was only a matter of time before Malcolm had to come up with a new idea, or a new toy, to satisfy his strange curiosity. On a pre-season tour, in Rotterdam, he came up with the brainwave of throwing in an almost unknown, well-travelled player, Barry Silkman, as a sweeper. He'd come from Plymouth, via Orient and Crystal Palace, as a winger! I soon let Malcolm know that it was the most ridiculous thing I had experienced in my life, and I thought if he carried on like this we were absolute certs for relegation in his first season as manager.

I was promptly hoicked around as being available for transfer and after being offered the player–manager's job at Blackpool and a possible playing job at Swindon, I hightailed it back to Lawrie McMenemy at Southampton – better the devil you know! At the time I thought perhaps it's wrong to think you can go back, but it worked out better than I could have ever hoped.

I was to have three more great years at Southampton, two years of European football and some great days with my Saints pals, Kevin Keegan and Alan Ball. I know it's important to win things, but it doesn't half help if your're enjoying life as well.

To sum up Malcolm Allison, he made his name at Manchester City as a great coach. Why did he make his name at City? The answer is that he had great players: the likes of Summerbee, Lee and Bell. That's what makes a good coach. This fellow called Tactics may be the most popular player in the country, but he never wins a game and he never scores a goal. Tactics are absolutely useless unless players believe in them and are prepared to work at them – and think that they are right. Quite simply, players win games not tactics.

In Malcolm's mind he had to be the one who was responsible for the team winning – not the players. The game had to be about Malcolm Allison, and that's why he never was what I would call a manager. He was a great talker and what he said, the majority believed. I was too long in the tooth for him to change me – thank goodness. He would never understand that you can't put square pegs in round holes. He wanted you to do something that was foreign to you when he should have been getting players to use their certain strengths. And what really did for him in the end was that all he kept buying were kids.

He knew he had a chance of changing youngsters because they are not set in their ways. But experienced pros would have none of it. I wasn't surprised when he got the sack, after I'd left. That old power struggle I've talked about had turned into a battle between Malcolm Allison and older players. And unless you are all together, there is only one loser – it was Malcolm Allison.

To this day there is only one thing holding back Manchester City, and that is their obsession about neighbours United. Instead of forgetting or ignoring United and getting on with their own job, they are looking over their shoulder all the time. What are *they* doing? What have *they* got that we haven't got? What can we do to be better than *them*? I say stuff United, think about being a great club in your own right. Never mind what United are up to. Get your own house in order.

I loved life in Manchester – regarding the city and the people everything was fine. My big mate socially was Asa Hartford, as you can probably gather from the odd escapade of ours. He's Scottish, and despite my suspicion about all things Gaelic I still think the occasional Scotsman is all right – as long as there isn't more than one in your company! One at a time they're great. Two or more and you've got a riot.

While I was at City, one of the funny stories concerned Scotland's World Cup blow up in Argentina in 1978. Both Asa and Willie Donachie from City were in the Scottish squad. What chaos it caused in City's Maine Road camp when poor old Willie Johnston was kicked out of the World Cup for taking a so-called illegal drug. There was absolute panic in the Manchester City dressing room when it was exposed, because the majority of our players had been taking the same thing for ages without even thinking that it could be illegal.

It wasn't a dangerous drug as we think of today, like cocaine or heroin. In fact, I think it was more for psychological benefit. After all, people often think if they are taking something it must be helping them to recover from a particular ailment. If players are having a bad time, they get some comfort from thinking they could run that bit more or be that much stronger. I can assure you that it wasn't even a so-called soft drug in my eyes let alone a hard drug. I wouldn't know, nor most players, what a hard drug is. But the World Cup business led to the physio emptying the medicine cupboards and throwing away everything that remotely resembled a tablet that could get us into trouble if drug tests were suddenly brought in.

Knowing poor Willie Johnston, I'm sure he didn't think twice when he took the tablets that got him kicked out. To have made him look like some kind of junkie was ridiculous and very sad. He was the fall guy.

Strangely enough, later on at Southampton I was one of the first players to be subjected to a routine drug test. I saw red, and refused. God, I'd been playing the game long enough without suspicion of being some pill head. I took it as an insult to my standing as a professional footballer and as a person that I should be checked for such things in a random way. Taking real drugs was against everything I've ever stood for or believed in. It causes so much pain and heartache to kids, it appals me. I'll always remember the lad from the FA saying: 'Well don't worry, you can always get someone else to pee in the bottle!' I found it quite humorous and replied: 'In that case I'd better do it myself, in case they are on something!' But seriously, I don't believe you can take the sort of drugs that are a blight on the lives of young people today and still be a top player. I know about steroids and unscrupulous athletes taking them for putting on bulk – but throwing the shot or the javelin wouldn't be much use to me. I don't believe that drug abuse is widespread in football, although you'll get some idiots in any walk of life. It would be much more of a hindrance than a help.

The only stimulant that I know players take regularly is booze. But that's invariably for celebrating or drowning your sorrows – no player could go out on the pitch and give of his best with say ten pints of lager inside him, it's not possible. There's far too much made of players having a drink the night before a game or indulging in sexual activity too near to the kick-off. They just join a long list of excuses for a player basically not being good enough.

7 · My England

I consider myself privileged to have played for the greatest manager England ever had – Sir Alf Ramsey. He not only put me on my way to five years and forty-six caps as an international, but he set impossibly high standards for those that followed him as England team manager.

I believe that England have never been quite the same, no matter how hard the likes of Don Revie, Ron Greenwood and currently Bobby Robson have tried. For one thing, I don't think that an England cap is the prized possession it once was. Under Sir Alf a cap had to be earned the hard way – since then they have been scattered about like confetti. But once you had earned your stripes with Sir Alf he stuck by you no matter what the outside pressures. Yes, he was aloof – but it was a fantastic strength because no one could make him change his course from his intended path.

Alf was a strange man in many ways, but he had a certain warmth and he got tremendous respect from anyone who played for him. He first picked me for the England Under-23 side (as it was in those days) and I got an insight into his character at the end of a tour we'd made to the USSR.

We had a reception in Kiev that turned into a party. There were some smashing lads in that squad like Frank Worthington, Kevin Keegan, Steve Perryman, Larry Lloyd and Peter Shilton. We had played well for a creditable draw and at the reception celebrated with plenty of the local Russian vodka. I got up and did my party piece, a song right for

'The greatest manager England ever had . . .'

a country boy, 'I rise at six and feed the chicks' and Frank did his Elvis Presley impression with 'Blue Suede Shoes'. We were eating on a balcony and Kevin Keegan knocked a drink off it, drenching someone down below. That caused one or two problems but we were just having a good time, nothing malicious, merely a bunch of young lads who were a bit rowdy. We got back to the hotel and there was a bit of a commotion about one of the players, Steve Perryman, getting his bedroom mattress turned over. He wasn't very happy and made a bit of noise knocking on our door. The next thing I knew Alf Ramsey had come into the room. My room-mate at that time was Derby County's John Robson, who so tragically developed multiple sclerosis later in his career. We had been carrying on the party in our room and Alf gave us a real dressing down.

I remember thinking: Oh, we're really in trouble here, we probably won't get picked for England again. But I shouldn't have worried because Alf, being the man he was, always picked his teams on ability. I survived that scare and became a regular player. I had nine Under-23 caps in all before stepping up to the seniors.

To get into Alf's senior England team, however, was the equivalent of breaking into the Bank of England – it was that hard. I can never forget my first call-up to the senior England squad. In those days we assembled at Hendon Hall, North London and I was so keen I must have been the first one there. Although I'd played regularly in the Under-23 side, this was my first time with the big boys, alongside the likes of Bobby Charlton, Geoff Hurst, Martin Peters and Bobby Moore.

I remember going into the reception area to be told, quite matter of factly, that I was rooming with 'Mr Banks'. I was so nervous waiting for the great Gordon Banks to come to the room. But not only was he a great player, he was one of the nicest people you could wish to meet – I never heard him say a bad word about anyone.

It's a sad thing now because all he ever wanted to do was

With Eric Martin, Southampton's goalkeeper from the 'Ale House' days.

Jim McCalliog has a word in my ear during the FA Cup semi-final against Crystal Palace in 1976.

The 1976 FA Cup final. (*Above*) Taking on Stewart Houston. (*Below*) Skinning Martin Buchan.

Southampton's FA Cup-winners.

Holding the Cup aloft, as Ossie and Lawrie look on.

Nicking the ball away from Clem – one of that over-protected species . . . goalkeepers.

Channon and Ball!

I've never been a great one for training ... and it shows in this warm-up for an international in the USSR in 1973.

One of the highs of Don Revie's England reign – after a victory over Italy in the American Bicentennial Tournament in 1976.

Introducing HM the Queen to the Football League team (*left to right*: Trevor Francis, Joe Royle and Steve Coppell) before the Silver Jubilee match in Glasgow.

Jubilation after scoring the first goal in England's 7–0 trouncing of the Austrians in 1973.

An aerial attack from Kevin and I in the 1976 international against Finland at Wembley.

stay in the game. He's only managed that in a limited capacity since the car crash that cost him one of his eyes. The strange thing about football is there seems to be little or no place for nice people.

Having met the legendary Gordon Banks, the nerves were still showing as I went downstairs to be asked by Franny Lee if I fancied a game of cards. Hurst and Peters were there as well and we settled into a game of seven card brag. You had to win both hands to take the pot and it was a fiver a time – for me at the time it was quite a bit of money. I didn't realize it would be as much as a fiver, but once you're in that's it – there was no backing down. You had to act 'big time', even if you were a first timer with the top men. I thought: 'What have I let myself in for here?' But I just about survived as I remember with my shirt intact. And I kept face in that all-important first meeting with England's finest.

Bobby Charlton was certainly one of the greatest players I ever faced at club level, although we never played together for England. But he was also one of the great all-time moaners. I remember playing for Southampton against Manchester United and I kicked him accidentally. Whinge? You've never heard anything like it – but a fine player for all that.

As an England new boy I looked up to him as I had done from my early days. I'm certainly not embarrassed about having heroes when I was a lad – that's the kind of thing that the game thrives on. That's what worries me today, whether the lads have got respect for the older pros – everyone wants to be jack-the-lad and that frightens me a bit.

The West Ham players Bobby Moore, Geoff Hurst and Martin Peters were fairly quiet lads who didn't say a lot, I recall. Alan Ball was completely different, always bubbly, always having something to say – and that comes through in his play and his lifestyle. He has never changed.

You tend to find that the strong characters in a party of players live off each other. There's always a response and a laugh and a joke flying about. Then the ones who are more shy tend to get together, but that's no different to life in general.

It was just over a year after the 1970 World Cup in Mexico that I made my full England début on 11 October 1972 at Wembley against Yugoslavia. The match ended in a 1–1 draw, with my Manchester City team mate-to-be Joe Royle scoring our goal.

Once you got into Alf's squad you knew you were going to get a fair crack. And if you were good enough then you would have the chance of a decent run in the team. It makes me laugh these days, players get picked for the squad on the Monday and ten days later they're an international. I can assure you when Alf was the manager you got picked for the squad, and then probably had to spend a year of England match nights just sat in the stands, not even in the sixteen as a substitute. He had a bloody, good long look at you and got you in a situation where you knew all the other players – it became like a club team. You were with them, you trained with them so all the complexes were gone, you weren't shy any more or frightened to take the micky out of other lads. It all added up to players feeling as though they were thoroughly involved. That's where Alf got his fantastic team spirit, and I can see how we won the 1966 World Cup. It's not how long you're together at a certain time that matters, it's that when you are together you feel comfortable with your fellow squad members. Managers say they don't get players together long enough for internationals. But to put it in perspective, Alf had his squads for much shorter periods than Bobby Robson. Even Ron Greenwood had England players for longer periods before games than Alf.

So I was at least twelve months in the England twenty-two, as it was in Alf's day, before I even looked like getting in the side. And the only reason I got a chance then was because there had been a lot of players dropping out because of club commitments. I was one of six new caps. It wasn't until the February, four months later, that I became an England regular. That is a sweet memory because I scored when we turned over Scotland 5–0 in their centenary match on their own ice-covered, Hampden Park pitch. If I loved to beat anyone it was them. The Scots have so much passion, and I admire them for that, but it didn't stop me hating them when we faced each other.

I then played the next four England games – only to be left out of the June, 1973 World Cup qualifying game we lost in Poland 2–0. Alf decided to play with an extra midfield man in Arsenal's Peter Storey and sacrifice one of the strikers – me. The shame about the Polish defeat was that with the team we had then, I'm convinced we could have gone on to win the World Cup, if we had but qualified for the finals. Alan Ball, Martin Peters and Bobby Moore were still going strong, Tottenham's Martin Chivers was in sharp form up front with me and Allan Clarke of Leeds. We had either Peter Shilton or Ray Clemence in goal with big Roy McFarland just in front – it was a good blend of players. I came back for England in our next game, a 2–1 win over the USSR in Moscow that I have always considered to be my best international performance.

It was after that game that Alf admitted to me he had made a mistake in not playing me in Poland. I always thought that was very big of him. He said it in his inimitable way: 'I'm sorry but I should have played you in Peo-land.' I kept playing for him then until he went.

The great thing about Alf was that everyone knew what they were doing. If you were with him, you were there because he wanted you to be there, and he thought you were good enough. He didn't have any doubts about his players. He knew what they could do and put them on the pitch in a situation where they would be able to play the game to the best of their ability. Alf didn't go on about tactics. Sure, he would go through the other team and say that this fellow has a good left foot – but he wouldn't go on about how to stop them. He'd say: 'You're here because you're the best in the country – you're internationals.' Alf more than repaid his country and his players more than repaid him. After he had gone I felt that too many England players didn't reach their full potential at international level. It was always going to be hard to produce a good international team after Alf because of the excellent way he shaped his teams. Of course, he made mistakes, like during the World Cup match in Leon, Mexico when he took off Bobby Charlton for Colin Bell and England went down 3–2 in extra time.

You got the impression with Alf that he didn't give a damn for the Press or the media as a whole. All he was interested in were his players and the way they performed. In hindsight, if he had handled the Press a bit better he would probably have still been manager of England today if he had wanted. There's no doubt that his downfall was his contempt for the media.

Just after Alf got the sack we went on a tour to East Germany, Bulgaria and Yugoslavia in the summer of 1974. The caretaker manager was good old Joe Mercer. He was brilliant, I don't think anyone else could have done the job that he did. Joe had a tremendous happy-go-lucky attitude towards it – and we got some great results for him with a draw in Leipzig, a win in Sofia and another draw in Belgrade. It was the tour on which Kevin Keegan got arrested in Yugoslavia. The last thing Joe needed was for something like that to happen because he wasn't a well man, with a slight paralysis down one side. He felt pretty rough on the tour, but bless him he saw it through. I've often seen him round the grounds over the past few years and it has surprised me how well he looked. He kept the team together through a really testing time.

In the airport at Belgrade Kevin Keegan got beaten up, it was a simple as that. It almost became an international incident at the time. It all happened over a U-shaped conveyor belt used for taking luggage off aeroplanes. Kevin had bought some fragile gifts that came through on the belt.

As his goods came round Kevin stepped over one package to get to another. As he did it must have looked as though he was standing on the conveyor belt. Suddenly a guard or a member of the secret police had grabbed him and started to push him about. Kevin tried to tell him or motion to him not to be so daft and the whole thing blew up. By then there were three people with their hands on him. I was next to them trying to calm down a situation that had got out of all proportion. But the three heavies manhandled him out of the baggage area with his arm behind his back and there was nothing anybody could do about it. We found out later he had been punched and generally done over – a right mugging – just because he was trying to get to one of his bags.

There was a players' meeting and we were all ready to go home. Nobody was drunk, there had been absolutely no trouble, but Kevin had suffered because of police-state methods. You couldn't reason with them or talk to them. Then good old Joe said: 'Listen lads, the only way you can show these people up is to get out there and give their team a bloody good hiding!' Well, we drew but we should have won. Malcolm Macdonald was clean through in the last minute and knocked the ball wide. But Kevin scored, that gave him a lot of satisfaction, and I did as well.

During that short space of time Joe did a great job, the main thing is that Joe Mercer had steadied the ship. He let players play and wasn't one of these managers who made it seem like a job of work – it was a fun thing, the way the game should be played. Today there are far too many managers who don't want players to do things instinctively, but just to do as they are told. Joe was a lovely romantic when it came to football.

It was almost inevitable that Don Revie would get the England job because of his club record with Leeds. I know that a lot of muck has been thrown at Revie over the last few years – and the way he ran out on England to pick up the desert gold may have been wrong – but I believe he still doesn't get the credit he deserves. I know he's got his enemies and a lot of people have fallen out with him, but for me his biggest mistake was in trying to keep everybody happy – the players, the media, the club managers. It was impossible.

Then there was the commercial side, as well, with which he insisted on getting involved. All this he may have done at Leeds over a period of time – but he tried to do it with England all in the space of a couple of years, with the World Cup thrown in for good measure.

I know Revie had this thing about organizing stupid little games to try and keep the interest of the players during rest times, like carpet putting, bowls and bingo, in order to kill the boredom. That was his way and he thought it would work for him. It didn't really, but I'll confess I played putting with him and it didn't do any harm. You weren't doing anything in the evening anyway and it provided the odd laugh – you didn't want to get knocked out of the competitions he organized in the first round.

I've got time for Don Revie, although I know a lot of people haven't. But when he first took over he said: 'You *will* be punctual, and you *will* call me boss.' In my opinion, that's all wrong. As he was England manager you'd address him like that anyway. You're talking about internationals, not slips of kids.

Then there was his famous get-together in Manchester of fifty-odd players – it was the biggest cockup ever, players came from all over the country and it turned into what must have been the biggest footballers' booze-up in history.

Can you imagine what it was like when Don Revie told us he wanted us all to get off to bed that Saturday night? We'd all been involved in League games and it's traditional as the night to let your hair down. His point was that he wanted us to go back to our club managers bright-eyed and bushy-tailed, so he thought an early night was in order – some chance! Any ordinary people visiting the hotel were in danger of being trampled in the rush as the boys raced out to play night games in pubs and clubs. You can imagine, it was like meeting old friends you don't normally see socially except at the odd annual dinner. I'm not saying that everyone got paralytic, but I'll bet the landlords and club owners of Manchester did a roaring trade that night.

We had the get together on the Sunday morning and then in the afternoon all went our separate ways back to our clubs. I still can't work out to this day what was the purpose of that meeting.

Revie was very money-conscious even then before he'd had a chance to dream of fortunes in the Middle East – but to be fair it didn't do the players any harm. We used to earn £60 for an international until Don got busy doing a deal with Admiral to supply the England kit – after that it was £100 basic and £200 for a win. It's only a little thing, but I don't think the £60 appearance money had been changed for years. He was very aware of the commercial aspect of qualifying for the World Cup and he fixed up an agent in Harry Swales who, I believe, is still involved with England. I'm sure the players would have made a lot more, if we had qualified for the World Cup.

Revie's famous dossiers, however, were a silly idea to me. They drove me mad. I always remember before an important World Cup qualifying game against Italy at Rome in November, 1976 there were a few of us playing cards in the hotel. It was about 11.30 at night and that well-known gambler Stan Bowles was in this particular card school when one of the lads called last hand. It was the night before the game and Stan pleaded: 'Come on lads, let's not finish just yet.' It wasn't that Stan couldn't bear to call it a day, believe me. His room mate was Dave Clement, that super right-back who was so tragically to commit suicide some years later. Stan explained: 'Dave is driving me mad. I can't go back to that room yet – he must have read his dossier six times.'

To an intensely caring person like poor Dave it was too much and he was desperate to take in what Revie had given him in the dossier. For the likes of Stan and myself we were quite happy to toss it aside and not bother. Our thinking was that no dossier could help us when we got out on the pitch. The dossiers really became an obsession with some who would take it too seriously and start believing they were facing some kind of supermen. That was a mistake when dealing with top-class and international players. It was different at Leeds where players grew up with his habits, and many wouldn't have known any different. But suddenly to try to drill mumbo-jumbo into the heads of experienced players who are set in their ways was wrong. Alan Ball, for one, couldn't stand it, and Alan Hudson was another. It didn't bother me one way or the other, because I never read them – perhaps that was largely down to my lack of education!

To be fair to Revie, perhaps it was up to the individual as to how he treated the dossier. If you wanted it, it was there. You can't fault Don for not covering every minor detail – thoroughness is no crime. The only trouble is that the lads were beginning to take it too seriously. These damn dossiers, along with bingo, bowls and putting were getting more publicity than the football. It was all blown up too much. Funnily enough, a couple of the putting tournaments became quite earnest events. It was the old competitive spirit coming out. I was absolutely useless at the putting, but I remember winning it one day. Revie and Keegan were the bookies and I took £250 off them! They quoted me at 25–1, which shows you what they thought of my prowess and I had a tenner on.

Keegan and Revie were quite close, especially as Kevin was England captain. And it was thanks to Revie that I eventually achieved what I regard as the greatest honour in the game – to lead my country.

I still think he made a mistake by getting rid of Alan Ball far too soon. Revie went through too many players, chopping and changing his England teams. It was completely the opposite to Sir Alf Ramsey. With Revie either your face fitted or it didn't – you were in or out. Frank Worthington was out almost as soon as Revie became England boss. Then Bally had a slight disagreement with him and he was chopped for good.

Alan Hudson was another who didn't last too long, despite his brilliant performance when we beat West Germany 2–0 in March, 1975 at Wembley. You only had to fall out with Revie and that was it. That was never Alf Ramsey's way.

Also I think Revie was guilty of pre-judging people, like Ron Greenwood was to do with me later when he took over. But I accept that's the sort of thing which happens – one manager likes you as a player, another doesn't.

Something happened between Hudson and Revie and that was a shame because we looked like having a fair side after the victory over West Germany. Hudson was in and then out – but not just out, it was off with his head, finished. Don was leaning over backwards to do what the Press wanted – they'd call for Supermac one week, Stuart Pearson another, and so on. Yet when he left out Kevin Keegan one time he got a dramatic answer. Kevin promptly got off the coach and headed for home. I didn't take him seriously at the time, but the next thing he'd upped and gone. However, it certainly did the trick for Kevin. Once he was reinstated he was never out of the side. For most players it would have gone against them with Revie, but not Kevin. Being the strong character he was, it definitely worked in his favour.

Revie's darkest hour came when we lost 2–0 in Rome, a vital World Cup qualifying match for us in November, 1976. He was distraught. However, I must say he made a real mess of that team selection. The blunder was in playing Brian Greenhoff, who was basically a back four player, in midfield. We were very weak in the middle of the park. But that day I developed an awful lot of respect for Stan Bowles. He had been brought in on a wave of heavy praise for his form with QPR at that time. Not only was Stan a very talented, skilful player but his attitude to the game was first class, and it needed to be on that day. He was such a good competitor.

It hurts me a bit when I think that Stan may be remembered only as something of a gambler. He may have been wild, but he was very exciting to watch, and there aren't many about today as good as he was. He was a first-class trainer with England and loved to play the ball. It was sad when the seedier parts of his life were brought up all the time. In the theatre or in films, if you are a good actor you get the job. But in football if you're a bit wild, even if you are the best, invariably they kick you out. That's a slur on our game and, more than that, a slur on the managers who don't persevere with special talent. That is my pet hate about managers. If a player has got the ability and is a bit different from the rest, so what? Life isn't about everyone being equal and everyone being treated the same. But that's what the majority of managers want today. They want everyone cloned out of the same mould.

After the Rome defeat we could tell Revie was very low and the following June we went on tour of South America, with his assistant, the late Les Cocker, in charge. We started against Brazil in Rio de Janeiro and Revie caught up with us in Argentina. Of course we were to learn later that Revie missed the first part of the trip because he was already having talks in Dubai and securing his future.

Revie had made his mind up that he wasn't going to end up a forgotten man with nothing, and he wanted to be richly recompensed. I wouldn't have done it that way and I reckon, given the opportunity again, neither would he. But at the time he probably felt his whole world had fallen apart. He'd been the brain behind Leeds and their rise to the top. He'd given it all up for England and it had never gone right for him. He was used to only having success and things going well. I just think he probably panicked. I don't feel it was premeditated. I think it was done rather quickly without thinking. If he'd had a chance to think it over again, I believe he would have done it differently. But he's paid his penalty with all the stick he has taken.

Revie departed in the summer of 1977. It was soon after we got back from South America that I got my move to Manchester City. The FA were trying to settle everything down and get in a man of integrity, not that I thought Revie lacked that quality. But it has to be said he was a bit ill-advised in some of the things he did. They ended up picking on Ron Greenwood – and they might as well have pointed a loaded gun at my head! As I was soon to find out, my England career was coming to an abrupt end.

Ron Greenwood just didn't fancy me. Why? I don't know, but I remember he started off by calling little meetings at different clubs. Manchester City were playing at West Ham so there were a few England candidates together. After the game he called us in to his old office, as he had been manager at Upton Park. He said that he'd been around to a few places and that some of the players seemed to think they were automatic choices for England. He said it in front of me and I've always thought since then that he'd got me down as one of those people who regarded himself as automatic. I'd been there for nearly five years. Perhaps I was over-sensitive, but after that when he named his first team two or three weeks later for Wembley in September – I wasn't in it.

There was a bit of a stir in the papers, with Mick Channon being left out for the first time in nearly five years. I played on the Saturday for Manchester City and scored two goals; we beat Norwich City 4–2. After the game there was a phone call asking me if I'd go down for the England game at Wembley against Switzerland as someone had dropped out injured. So I went down, but for the first time I didn't feel part of it. It was a strange feeling. I was put in the team, but only for half a game. He took me off at half-time for Manchester United's Gordon Hill and that was it, the end of me as an England player.

I don't think Greenwood disliked me. It wasn't a personal thing I'm sure – he just didn't fancy me as a player. The only thing I found peculiar was: if he didn't fancy me, why did he suddenly call me up, and then promptly pull me off after forty-five minutes? I suppose I had been built up in the Press as the axed England man who had scored two goals. Greenwood asked me to play wide, but I just went where I wanted to. It was 0–0 at half-time. I wasn't playing particularly well, but then I don't think the team was either. The game ended up goalless. I never spoke to anyone about it. Yes, I was annoyed because I believed I was still good enough, but without that attitude you shouldn't be playing the game in the first place.

Greenwood, for me, didn't radiate any feeling of great enthusiasm. He was methodical, yes, but there was no warmth. You didn't feel he had any passion about him. Of course he does love the game, but in my opinion he had lived off that greatly hyped-up business about West Ham being the academy of football. You'd have thought no one else had ever kicked a ball if they hadn't passed through the West Ham club. The whole country was a little bit brainwashed by that. He was a lucky man, he had some great players. He became a good manager at West Ham because he had some terrific talent. But I stress that I thought he was a good manager with great players!

The only disappointment I had with Ron Greenwood came at a later stage over a television appearance. As I wasn't to be in the England team any more I was asked to go on Independent Television's panel of so-called football experts. It was in the European Championships of 1980 and we were playing Italy in Turin. He had picked Gary Birtles for his first game. I couldn't believe he could toss in an almost untried player like that for such an important game. With eight or nine Juventus players on their home pitch, the task was going to be pretty daunting. I've played there and experienced it. So I said my piece on television, always believing you should say what you think.

Ron had agreed he would come into the television studio later to talk about the game, which England then lost 1–0. But by all accounts he'd spoken to his wife on the phone and she had said I'd had a go at him because of the team he picked – and he refused to come in. That disappointed me because I only gave an opinion, that was just my thinking. Surely he was above Mick Channon, the footballer or TV pundit. I think he should have come in and explained why he picked the team he did. If he couldn't face up to his critics he didn't deserve to be England manager for me. As a footballer I've had to live with criticism all my life. I've had all the praise and the pats on the back. I loved all that. But I had to be big enough to take the kicks in the pants as well.

Looking at the England team of today with Bobby Robson in charge, I'm optimistic about what the future holds. We've got world-class players even now. The only thing that bothers me is that we are a little bit erratic. I believe Robson has got problems with his back four. In midfield and up front we've got players who can compare with any country in the world. His England teams remind me of the ones he had at Ipswich, always well-disciplined with strong lads at the back, aggressive, competitive and very physical. Ipswich always like to get the ball forward as early as possible, which is great for forwards – but it's how you get it forward that counts. The spare man at the back has to be comfortable on the ball. If you get it forward early with control and you have good players up front, then you can play. But hump the ball forward early without too much thought and all that happens is it comes straight back on your defence. Whether Bobby can take things that little bit further and use the skills of players like Glenn Hoddle and Steve Williams – yes, Williams despite what some people think of him – remains to be seen.

England have already got a world-class midfield man in Bryan Robson, such a great competitor and a good finisher with a natural instinct for goals. Robson's not delicate and able to do the same things as Hoddle, he can't beat a man like Chris Waddle, he's not as good at shielding a ball as Peter Reid, who holds things together. But his running and enthusiasm cut teams apart – he goes into areas where he can do real damage to the opposition.

With Steve Williams, I know he didn't have the best of starts at Arsenal after he left Southampton. But it's not unusual for a player to look bad with them. For a parallel, look at me and my disaster at Manchester City, where Denis Tueart and Joe Royle also struggled for a time. The Pole, Kaziu Deyna, one of the most capped players in the world, was another Maine Road flop for a long while.

I must admit I'm very concerned about Don Howe being Robson's assistant. I didn't rate Howe as manager of Arsenal.

He became a good coach, as the Arsenal double-winning team revealed, but what great players he had to work with: Frank McLintock, Charlie George, George Graham, John Radford, Geordie Armstrong, Peter Simpson and Bob McNab. They were all top-class players – though solid and workmanlike as a team, maybe. You couldn't say that anyone of those would fail to get in the Arsenal side of today.

On the England playing side I still think too many caps are lobbed out to players. Bobby Robson, Don Revie and Ron Greenwood have all fallen into the same trap. Between them they have devalued England caps so much we are almost getting to the stage where you can buy them in Woolworth's.

8 · A Dell Boy Again

I couldn't wait to return to Southampton and become a Dell boy again. I was going back to a manager who had had shortcomings regarding the game when I was first there. But when Lawrie McMenemy bought me back from Manchester City for £175,000, he was so powerful that I called him 'The Ayatollah'. He had learned fast and come a long way.

The first I knew that I could be on my way from Maine Road was when Tony Book – by then he had the title of general manager – said I could go to Swindon. My first reaction was: I can do better than that for myself. It was an ambitious move by Swindon's manager Bobby Smith, who knew me in the north-west when he was boss at Bury.

I just had to leave City after having a row with Malcolm Allison. Then came a very interesting offer from Third Division Blackpool to become their player–boss. I remember going into their boardroom at Bloomfield Road, after having slept on their offer. It had driven me crazy because I knew I could still play. I was only coming-up thirty then. I'll never forget being invited into their board meeting and seeing the old chairman, who wore a jet black toupee that was the most obvious wig you've ever seen. I said to them: 'Gentlemen, before we go any further it's very kind of you to invite me here and to give me an interview with the chance of a job. I'm very flattered to have been invited along to an interview. But I feel it's in the best interests of Blackpool and Mick Channon that I don't take the job. I feel I can play for a few more years and it's important you carry on with your job of finding a manager, while I carry on playing.'

Suddenly the chairman jumped up and exclaimed: 'Oh, young man, I've been involved as a director in football for twenty-odd years and that is the most impressive speech I've ever heard from anyone. Are you sure we can't talk you round? We'd love you to come and watch us tonight at Bury.' I told them that it was very kind of them and by all means I would go and watch them. I did, we shook hands on very good terms and that was that. So I could have had the job at Blackpool.

Then, about a week later, Allison told me that McMenemy wanted to speak to me. Southampton were playing against Manchester United on the Saturday and Lawrie had asked whether I would go and see him. I certainly was a bit surprised, because we'd had our disagreements over the years. But sometimes you don't appreciate people until they're not there. That probably applied to Lawrie just as much as me! Normally I would say it's wrong to go back, but the circumstances were a bit different in this case. I was going back to people I knew. I was convinced I'd be able to get on and play the game as I wanted to. I had to give myself the chance to get on the stage again.

No sooner had I arrived back at The Dell than Alan Ball was in England again after having played very successfully for Vancouver in the North American league. So, as one-time great pals in the England squad, we met up again for three smashing years with Southampton. We qualified for Europe every season. Then to cap it all, the season after I returned McMenemy signed up Keegan, my old England room mate and by this time a horse-racing partner as well.

In fact, it was a racing date that made it appear as though I'd snubbed his razzamatazz homecoming from Hamburg, which had been laid on by Lawrie for the maximum effect in newspapers and television.

The season before Kevin arrived Southampton had a successful time, qualifying for Europe. I still hadn't moved house from Manchester and I remembered going home for the weekend and McMenemy saying he wanted me back on the Monday morning. Normally I would never come back until the Tuesday unless we had a midweek game or some special trip laid on. He said: 'You know something exciting is going to happen.' To be fair I didn't have a clue what he was talking about. I hadn't spoke to Kevin for a while because he was in Hamburg.

I remembered that a couple of months earlier Lawrie had asked me about Kevin and I never thought anything more about it. I had given him Keegan's home number in Hamburg, so obviously Lawrie must have thought that Kevin would have told me what was going on. I didn't know a thing. On the Sunday I phoned up Lawrie and told him I wouldn't be back the next day because I had a horse running at Wolverhampton. He said to me: 'You know I'm signing Kevin tomorrow, don't you?' I said: 'No I didn't know – but I do now.' He said that he wanted me and everyone else there because it was going to be such a big occasion. I said: 'I can see Kevin the rest of the year – I won't be able to see my horse run!' So I went to Wolverhampton. I think I got my priorities right!

So Lawrie had the big Press conference and like some grand magician pulling a prize out his hat, he produced Kevin Keegan. Everyone was there apart from me, his big England mate and horse-racing companion. But it didn't matter to me if Lawrie had been signing the best player in the world, the only help he'd be to me was on the pitch!

Although Keegan took the place by storm as the biggest personality again in English football, his first year at Southampton wasn't a very good one. A lot of things went wrong, but the club got into Europe once more.

It was the next season that we looked to have cracked it. We played some great stuff and went several points clear at the top of the First Division.

That was around April time when we'd played a few more games than everybody else. We were due to go away to Notts

The conjuring-up of Kevin

County and then on to Coventry. They were both struggling teams. I remember going into the dressing room and saying something like: 'We're four points clear at the top of the First Division, I know we've played several games more than the next team but we've got two away games now and one of them against real strugglers. We're 16–1 for the championship.' We had a players' pool going with a few quid in the kitty and I talked the lads into having £1,000 on us at 16–1. The only person who wasn't there was Chris Nicholl, who went back to be manager of the club last year. I don't think he would have had a bet. But £1,000 between the pool was less than £100 apiece so we weren't talking particularly big money. However, I remember the riot it caused, because we only drew at Notts County and lost at Coventry. My name was mud. If we'd won those two we would probably have been a 3–1 shot. But that's it. Unless you believe in something, you can never do it – and I'm sure there were players in our team who thought we couldn't win it. So we had done our grand. But I still thought it was a punt worth taking. Bally was straight along with me, Kevin agreed and we talked a few of the rest of them round. Chris Nicholl wasn't there, as I said, so I voted him in!

They were three blinding years for me back at Southampton when I really enjoyed my football again. We were a good attacking side and The Dell crowds used to average 22,000 – not bad when the ground capacity was only 24,000. The attraction wasn't just Kevin, although he was a great draw, it was the football we played. In every game there seemed to be three or four goals at least. It was excitement guaranteed. That was the year I scored the ITV goal of the season. The build-up to the goal was great, not just my finishing – and it was against Liverpool which made it a bit more special.

At that time, the value for money which supporters had out of watching us was top class. We were real crowd pleasers. It was a nicely balanced side with David Armstrong joining us from Middlesbrough and then making the England team and we had bright-as-a-button youngsters really making their mark like Steve Williams. Nick Holmes was his ever-reliable self and at the centre of defence we had Chris Nicholl.

When Chris was a player I certainly couldn't fault his professionalism. He was a great trainer and his work rate was high. But I always felt he held Southampton back. He was a defender who would never push up enough because he didn't like taking chances. But by dropping off, as he often did, he gave opposing players with lots of ability a great deal more room to operate in. He would play people onside and give top players the time and space they needed, instead of denying them those precious football commodities. I remember arguing and rowing with him plenty of times about it.

It wasn't just me, because Bally and Keegan gave him plenty of stick as well. 'Chris, you've got to push up,' we'd say. But he'd have none of it saying things like: 'I've been playing the game for a long time this way,' in that dour northern accent of his. He drove us mad.

Chris stood for almost everything in the game that I don't like. So it's ironical that he's now manager of the club that made me into a good player and gave me the values I've always kept in the game. But I suppose there is room for his type of player. We got over Chris's approach at The Dell because we could overrun most teams there, but away from home, because he would hang back, we handed the advantage in time and space to play to the home team. Chris could never be composed and comfortable on the ball, bringing it away himself. He wasn't skilled enough for that.

A player I did really get on with at the time was the Yugoslav, Ivan Golac. He had a lot of skill and we had a fine understandng down the right. He was a good defender who could attack. One of Lawrie McMenemy's quotes on him was: 'Yes, I thought my right-winger had an excellent game, the trouble is he's supposed to be my right-back!'

There's no doubt, however, that the player I was closest to was Kevin Keegan. We had been firm friends and room mates with England before he arrived at Southampton, so it was a real bonus when he became club mate as well. It just happened that we palled up together with England. And the friendship was confirmed when we owned the racehorse Man on the Run together. We had been two of the seniors who were established England players during the change from the Sir Alf Ramsey era to Don Revie's reign.

During our early international days Kevin and I used to send a fellow called Hector McDonald away for his holidays every year, after our trips to West Lodge Park in Hertfordshire for England get togethers. By the way, Hector was the local bookmaker!

Kevin started to take an interest in the horses when I had bred Man on the Run. I sold him a share – probably the worst investment he's ever made! But seriously Man won six races for us and we had an awful lot of fun with him. Horses can be a nightmare if you haven't got a genuine interest in them, but we went on from there and we still own a few horses together now.

As a player Kevin had a sensational rise to fame from Scunthorpe, going almost into the Liverpool first team where he made a big impact immediately. His dedication and work rate were extra special.

A good example of the huge effort Kevin put in came after England training sessions. The rest of us would flop on to the coach wanting to get back to the hotel for a shower, but he would always be the last one on board. There was always one more shot, corner or free-kick he wanted to take or work on. He'd always be messing around with a football. Things never came easily to Kevin and he'd be the first to admit it, but I noticed right from the early England days that he was a very bad loser and that's where his fierce competitive spirit came from.

Kevin had a very strong personality and it was during his second season at Southampton that I could see things coming to a head between him and Lawrie McMenemy. It was so similar to the situation between Terry Paine and Lawrie during my first spell at Southampton. The big difference this time, however, was that Kevin Keegan was by no means on the way out, like Terry had been.

Both Kevin and Lawrie were used to getting their own way, and a big bust-up between them was inevitable. We played Wolves in a Bank Holiday game towards the end of the season and got a rare home beating. We knew we had played badly and when Lawrie came in he said that we were useless and added: 'You lot didn't try today.' One of the lads said something, so did Kevin and then Lawrie added: 'That includes all of you'.

All of a sudden Kevin snapped and said: 'What do you mean I didn't try? That's one thing I've always done right through my career.' The trouble was that Kevin's pride had been hurt. But I still think Kevin was wrong. McMenemy had said something in the heat of the moment, the sort of thing that happens a thousand times in dressing rooms after a bad match. The manager is entitled to have his say afterwards, especially after you've had a good beating at home and his first reaction is bound to be: 'You've let me down, you didn't try.' In hindsight you realize it's only a heat of the moment thing. But Kevin took it personally as though the criticism was aimed at him.

Lawrie has got a very quick wit, he picks up on things straight away and hits you verbally. He's a very intelligent man who puts his words together and knocks people back. Perhaps that's why it was no real surprise to me when I heard he'd had that dressing room bust-up with Mark Wright during the 1985–6 season and he was pushed into the showers.

We were due to play at Swansea on the following Monday after the Wolves defeat. But Kevin had said that he was finished and he'd never play for McMenemy again. He had stormed home in that mood on the Saturday. He certainly didn't arrive at the team's hotel with the rest of us and it wasn't until about five o'clock that he turned up. He played that night, but the damage was done. They never spoke to each other after that.

The split was unavoidable, the old clash of personalities, with both of them bidding to be Mr Southampton. Lawrie was striving to impose his authority and although there was no way Kevin wanted to be the boss, he couldn't take being treated a certain way by the manager. Kevin took things too much to heart. Yet if I had worried about half the things that were said to me, I'd have never lasted half as long in football as I have. Bally was much the same.

Both McMenemy and Keegan had become too big – there was only room for one of them. It was from that time onward that I called Lawrie the 'Ayatollah'. He wanted to rule and that was it. He was *the* man and nothing or nobody would alter that.

If Kevin's flare-up with McMenemy hadn't happened when it did, I'm sure it would have come at some other time. Kevin will put his all into something for two or three years, then he'll want a change, another challenge. He can't settle, he likes to go in and do something – then move on. He did the same thing at Liverpool, Hamburg and Newcastle. He made himself a great player, but he always knew if he had outstayed his welcome.

Kevin could certainly have his rows with his fellow players as well. And Steve Williams was made for a confrontation with Kevin.

Steve, even then, was a cocky little so-and-so – but he could play. Steve has always wanted to be the best player at whichever club he's at. And in those days he had some fair competition with Keegan, Ball and myself. Steve Williams was just a young lad who had come into the team and it gave him a bit of a persecution complex. So he was always ripe for a ruck and I'll never forget him turning on Kevin one day and saying: 'Who the hell do you think you are?' Keegan rounded on him and replied: 'I'm something you'll never be, son.' Steve would gladly fight the world if he had to and it was a very abusive argument. Steve didn't become a really good player until Bally, Kevin and myself had all left Southampton.

I had my bust-ups with Steve as well. He always thought he was the greatest player and he certainly blossomed when the golden oldies moved on – perhaps it was because he had the extra responsibility. He was a fierce competitor but he wanted to be top man before his time. I saw a lot of myself when I was a young lad in him, impatient to get to the top quickly. There's nothing wrong with that.

One night at The Dell we played Arsenal, the club Steve eventually joined. I can certainly be aggressive in the way I play the game, though I don't go out of my way to kick anyone. The only time I have done it was on this night.

The game had boiled up after a ball broke between England left-back Kenny Sansom and Steve Williams. Steve might have gone over the top, so they started to have a bit of a barney. Sansom was mouthing off and I told Steve to get out of it. But then Kenny piped up: 'Hey you little . . ., who the hell do you think you are?' Stevie just shrugged his shoulders, but then Sansom added: 'How many caps have you got?' I went mad because Kenny Sansom had only just got in the England team and gained three or four caps. So I retorted: 'And how many of them fit you, Kenny?' So when the ball came near me and Kenny, I went out of my way to kick someone for the only time in my life. But that really did annoy me at the time, you don't say things like that. The likes of Kevin Keegan or myself would have been far more entitled to sneer something like that, but neither of us would have dreamed of it. I hope it's not something that Kenny does these days because he's a good player who doesn't need such nonsense. I often wondered, after Steve Williams went to Arsenal, how he and Kenny got on together as club mates, because it was an unpleasant incident that I haven't forgotten.

Kevin Keegan said to me after his row that he thought Steve would never be a good player. I disagreed. And even though Steve had his problems with Arsenal I'm sure he can make another England career for himself.

9 · The Other Side of the Cameras

I regard myself as extremely fortunate to have got involved with television as a so-called expert. It's meant I've been at World Cups and European Cups, I've travelled extensively and been able to see England play regularly.

I know people will say that it's very easy to sit back and be an armchair expert. But if you genuinely care about the game and how England play in particular, you are always a critic. I am aware that I'm labelled as being outspoken, but when England do well I'm one of the first to praise them. I'm one of England's biggest fans – and that's probably why I am critical at times. It's why I will question Bobby Robson's team selection just as I used to do to Ron Greenwood's choice (even though Ron didn't like it at all).

When I was at Norwich I remember bumping into Bobby Robson in the car park after a game and I congratulated him on a good England performance in the week. I said to him: 'The only reason I have a go at you on occasions is that I want us to be the best because that would be beneficial to our game.' He understood.

I'm no different from everybody back at home watching their football on television. I want the team to win, and if they are not playing well and not doing the right thing, then I become frustrated. That's because I know they can do better. What worries me about the England side is I know we've got better players than we produce at international level.

I learned, through playing for England, that we are a far better team when we are playing abroad and not fancied. We're never better than when we are knocked down. It's the English mentality at work. If we've got something to really get stuck into, there's nobody in the world better at it.

England didn't get beaten in the World Cup finals in Spain, even though we were a bit negative, which was down to Greenwood and, in particular, coach Don Howe. The team had three managers out there, Greenwood, Howe and Bobby Robson, who was then helping out. My biggest criticism of England in Spain was: who is running the show? Who do the players listen to?

When it came to the biggest game, they didn't pick our best team. I know Trevor Brooking and Kevin Keegan had been unfit, but if I ever become a manager I will always pick the best players available to represent me, especially when it came to the most important game in a competition. I have to say that I believe Ron Greenwood, or Don Howe, bottled it when it came to a team selection. For me, the team in Spain had a strong flavour of Don Howe about it, and I regard him as a very negative football thinker. He may be a great coach, he may set things out well enough, but there's more life in a glass of Andrews' than in many of his football teams.

I was very critical of England's management on television at the time. And once you criticize, people are looking for you to do it all the time. Brooking and Keegan had declared themselves fit – and that should have been good enough. I've played over 700 senior games, but if I had waited until I was fully fit each time I wouldn't have reached 200. You forget niggling problems; pick your best players; put them on the park – and hold your hands up. You've more chance of winning with your best players than your more ordinary ones, but by the time Brooking and Keegan were introduced it was too late.

My small-screen involvement really began when the television people liked the audience reaction to various interviews I gave during my own England days and they began to use me more on the Saturday lunch-time spots. People liked to take the mickey out of my accent, but at least it got me noticed. I've always been somebody who speaks his mind and I like to think that's a main reason why they wanted me – especially on ITV.

Certainly the TV lads are a great bunch of people to work for. At London Weekend Television I have a really good relationship with the production team led by Jeff Foulser and the top man John 'Brommers' Bromley. And, of course, commentator Brian Moore is a valued friend.

There's always a laugh and a joke, and when the World Cup comes together the LWT crowd put on a great team effort themselves. Everyone works very hard to bring out the programme, but they also have a lot of fun.

As far as the current crop of England players is concerned I think they have accepted me as a TV person – they know what they are going to get. They set their own standards, I don't do that for them. And don't forget I've been used to playing against them most weeks. I know how good or bad they are: I do understand a few of their problems. My inside knowledge helps my assessment of players.

Take Chris Waddle of Spurs, for example, who has been trying to make an England breakthrough to a regular place. I knew him when I was at Newcastle for a brief spell and I know one thing now – he'll never achieve greatness as a player at Spurs. He's a front runner who needs to be completely isolated, like he was at Newcastle. He needs to be put in one-against-one situations. But in a team like Spurs, who enjoy so much control of the ball, he only gets it when the opposing team are set. He's not the most intelligent player in the world, but he does have tremendous natural ability. He couldn't think his way out of a problem, he has to do it instinctively.

On the other hand I like the way Kerry Dixon has been

brought on as a player at Reading and Chelsea. He's been used the right way, and he's become a far better player than he's given credit for. He can hold things up even though his first touch isn't the best. That might come – a lot of it is to do with confidence. I do know what makes players like Waddle and Dixon tick.

Quite often I feel that England players are used in the wrong areas. I think I'm quite qualified enough, for instance, to stand up and say that John Barnes is often playing full-back. He's so far back from his winger's position that there's no other description for him. Basically he's a front man who should be pushed forward to feed off someone. All he seems to do, quite often, is stand ten yards in front of the left-back, Kenny Sansom, and get the ball. Barnes could become one of the best players in the world – he scored that great solo goal against Brazil. But at international level you've got to be able to think and understand how to get yourself regularly into good positions. The kid can't do it yet, but he's still very young.

I wouldn't have either Waddle or Barnes as my England wide man – he would be Trevor Steven. Trevor might not be quite as exciting as the other two, but he does think about the game. And I reckon he'll score far more goals than the other two. He's a tricky player, but you know what you're going to get when you put him on the pitch. You don't with Waddle or Barnes.

So there again, I've been critical – just as I can be on television – but I'm not talking about Chris Waddle as a person, or John Barnes for that matter. I'm talking about them as footballers. Chris Waddle is a lovely lad, but when you are a critic or a commentator, if you've got an opinion, you have to cut yourself off from thinking about a player in personal terms. As a footballer someone can be useless; as a person he can be great. But I reserve the right to have my say about his football ability.

Too many players can't take a straight-talking opinion about themselves. Football is about points of view and I've had to prove people wrong in my career. I've been written off three times at least and come right back. Southampton gave me a free the second time around, then Newcastle didn't keep me very long and I was going to retire at Bristol Rovers. Yet I ended up with a Milk Cup-winners' medal at Norwich before they turfed me out – only to go chasing trophies again at Portsmouth.

Footballers should remember that all we are is a commodity. When we are no longer useful we get thrown in the dustbin. I've been well paid all my life to play and I'm not about to start crying if I'm chucked out.

Is it a crime if a newspaper reporter says that Mick Channon is over the top? Of course it's not. Nor even: Mick Channon isn't a good player. If you worried about that kind of thing all your life you wouldn't go outside your front door.

It saddened me that in the 1985–6 season Gary Bailey decided he should go to the Players' Union to complain about certain remarks I made about him in the Press. I also said that I thought Norwich's Chris Woods would make a better England goalkeeper, and I haven't changed my mind about that.

I got a letter back from the Professional Footballers' Association secretary Gordon Taylor saying he was sure the Press had exaggerated it and I hadn't said all these things. But next time I saw Taylor I told him straight: I *did* say those things. And I'll go on permanent record now to say that I think Bailey has cost Manchester United trophies. To my mind he lost them the 1983 Milk Cup final against Liverpool. But that's my view, my opinion, nobody else's.

I just don't happen to think Gary Bailey is world class. Peter Shilton is a great goalkeeper for England, but Chris Woods could also do the job. Chris is potentially the best, but he's a 'confidence' player. He's better on crosses than Shilton, but he's got a soft side to him that makes him want to be liked all the time. You can't go through life always being liked by everybody; nobody can. It's dog eat dog, especially in the competitive world of football.

I'm afraid my former Southampton colleague and another England man, Mark Wright, can't take very much criticism either. He's twenty-two – a beginner in football terms – but after Lawrie McMenemy dared to have a go at him in that famous half-time incident in the showers, who would want to be his manager? Nobody, I would think, unless they can swim!

Rather than worry what Mick Channon or an old player has to say about them, I would have thought they had enough on their plate getting on with their own jobs.

Another player I don't think takes kindly to criticism is Trevor Francis, who for me was never worth a million pounds. He's a very moody type of lad who wants everything his own way. To a certain degree he's had just that. He's only had to work once in his life – that was when he went to Brian Clough at Nottingham Forest. Everywhere else he's been wrapped in cotton wool.

Francis seems to be nearly always injured and wants to play only when he feels like it. In my opinion he's been useless for England. His contribution to the England team has been negligible to be generous to him.

All credit to Cloughie for getting Francis to play to his strengths. I don't particularly like the way Cloughie talks down to players because I think they should be allowed to have their own opinions and be able to stand up to managers. Players have got a right to question the manager – they are the ones who are playing the game.

Francis scored the winning goal in the 1979 European Cup Final for Forest against Malmo from a midfield position. It was Clough's shrewdest move to play him on the right side of midfield so he didn't have an awful lot of defensive duties to do yet he could use that pace of his down the right. Francis wasn't that good with his back to goal but he had lightning acceleration and could go by people.

Of course, it wasn't Trevor's fault that he was a million-pound player. He didn't set the fee, and nobody can take away his ability – but I never saw him as a great player. At

Birmingham he was a bright light in an ordinary team, a bit like myself at Southampton at one time. He was the one spark with the turn of pace that could get Birmingham out of trouble almost single-handed. But there again, he was always injured. Cloughie made Francis's name and after a player has been transferred for a million, people begin to believe most of what they read about him. He was a luxury at Manchester City – and he's been a luxury for England. That's my honest opinion and it's the kind of viewpoint I would put over on television, and I'll continue to speak my mind on the box as long as I'm asked.

10 · Lawrie McMenemy

In my view Malcolm Allison has been highly overrated as a manager. He was on one big ego trip. The only thing which mattered was that Big Mal had done this or that. The last straw for me was that occasion in Rotterdam pre-season when he played Barry Silkman as sweeper.

So I played a few games when City came back to England, but the fact loomed large that Malcolm and I had rowed. It wasn't long before he told me that Lawrie McMenemy wanted to see me.

I met Lawrie at Mottram Hall, a country-house-type hotel in the Cheshire countryside. I'd been away from Southampton for two years. But when I went back there's no doubt about it – McMenemy was now the 'Messiah'. He was *the* man, who had pretty well got Southampton sorted out. He had got them back into the First Division, and by then had got rid of the likes of Peter Osgood and Ted McDougall. Alan Ball had been in Vancouver and Kevin Keegan had yet to arrive.

Lawrie McMenemy had got Southampton exactly as he wanted it. He's a very clever, shrewd man. You have to hand it to him. There's no doubt that given the time and the money he will get a club right. However, he has got to be the boss in every way.

When I went back to The Dell he had pruned away the wild lads: those players who were inconsistent, those who might question him and the ones who wouldn't do things the way he wanted them to. All he really lacked in the team then was experience. He needed quality players, so he got me and then Bally came back from Vancouver almost at the same time. Southampton were more than £100,000 to the good over my move, having sold me for £300,000 and got me back for less than £200,000.

I celebrated my homecoming by helping Southampton to beat Spurs 5–2. The fans were pleased to see me back. I've always had a good relationship with supporters at The Dell and it was to lead to another very happy spell for me there. The mountain had come back to Mohammed.

Bally and I were certainly strong characters who would have our say – but we wouldn't question McMenemy's authority. That's why he was happy to have us with him again. And he knew that we could still do a job for him. The two of us were fortunate that, as seasoned professionals, we could still operate at the top level, whereas Peter Osgood, as I've said before, reached his peak at around twenty-four and by thirty couldn't keep up the standard needed. It wasn't that Ossie didn't train – he was a hard worker – he just couldn't play in the First Division any more. I'm a lucky lad in that I've been able to last longer, but that's in your physique – the way you're put together.

Bally was getting on but he could run all day – he runs in marathons now – and in the middle of the park he was a tough little competitor.

McMenemy was very good at taking experienced players and squeezing them, like an orange, to keep getting something out. McMenemy knew that it's the experienced players who make the team tick, while younger players have highs and lows. It was fascinating to see McMenemy operate at this stage, after being there in my first spell when he arrived.

Quite frankly in those early day he was, in my opinion, tactically inept. But by the time I returned he had progressed and he had learned in the game through working with good players like Bally and myself, Peter Osgood and Ted MacDougall. He was a good listener and he got something out

'Lawrie could squeeze experienced players and still get something out'

of every player who passed through his hands. I still used to disapprove of a lot of things that he did. He used to rule by fear with a lot of the kids, who were frightened to death of him. It was martial law – they had to be in by nine o'clock and were fined if they were late, the baths had to be shining clean, the showers immaculate, the toilets spotless. It was real Army-style discipline, which I suppose shouldn't have been surprising with McMenemy's guardsman's upbringing. (Of course the place should be spick and span, but I believe it's not a job that should be done by the club's apprentices.)

I'm a great believer in personal freedom and comfort in dress and I used to question Lawrie's stiff rulings at times. He said to me that he always liked to see players coming in wearing collar and tie. He didn't like players to wear jeans or seeing them unshaven. That's fair enough, but I'm not sure it should be the rule. I think it's right that if you are travelling away you should be smart. I can also appreciate him wanting to start young kids in the right way. But I know that his coaching staff were frightened of him. If, for instance, a photographer came down to take a picture of a player, they wouldn't allow him into the ground until it had been cleared with McMenemy. But that was his rule and he was fierce about how his club should be run.

Out on the pitch the good, experienced players dictated the way we played. I would love to take credit for that but to be fair, McMenemy put the team together. It was his team and basically they didn't need to be coached. I'm sure McMenemy enjoyed it because we were always good for a few goals at The Dell – if we didn't knock in three, four or five there was something wrong.

Of course, McMenemy *did* have disciplinary problems with the infamous UEFA Cup trip to Sweden, but that was long after I'd left the first time. I remember McMenemy saying to me much later: 'I've had the biggest rascals in my life playing for me here: they would always be going out for a drink and a bloody good time. I've had the MacDougalls, the Osgoods, the Steeles, the Channons, the McCalliogs and the Balls. I knew you were out having a good time, but I could go to bed and wake up the next morning in the sure knowledge that you'd be there ready to go home again. But the young lads, they can be the nicest people in the club who would never question me, yet I never know what to expect. There's always trouble.'

So there's a lot to be said for the older lads who wouldn't hide anything. You knew they'd look forward to a good drink after a hard game abroad but you also knew they could manage themselves.

I never tried to socialize with Lawrie away from The Dell because I've always been a great believer that a manager stays a manager outside the confines of the club and there always has to be that area between boss and employee. Man to man I found him a smashing bloke who could be very generous, but there are definitely two sides to him.

If you get him on his own he's quite a different person to when the television cameras are switched on or the Press are around him. I believe he's an excellent manager, even though I call him 'The Ayatollah'. Certainly he was good for me. He was helpful to all the experienced players, including the ones who came later like Mick Mills and Joe Jordan, and by no means least Peter Shilton. We all gave him something – and in return he gave us two or three extra years on our careers at the highest level.

It's been whispered often enough that McMenemy is money orientated – the same was said about Don Revie. (Coincidentally, it has been rumoured that Revie was the man who put Lawrie in for the Southampton job originally.) But if it's a crime to earn money, then I'm guilty as well. Whatever Lawrie McMenemy has earned he's worked for.

I know the club has made money out of taking teams abroad for prestigious friendlies. In fact, one of my most amusing memories about the big man concerns one trip abroad that I was extremely keen to miss.

It was during my second year back at The Dell that Keegan arrived and things really took off – in more ways than one.

It was a case of have boots, will travel. With Kevin's hefty wages to be paid, it meant we were forever jumping in a plane to go off for a friendly somewhere, with Keegan the kind of attraction for which other countries and foreign clubs would pay dearly to see. Malaysia, America, Saudi Arabia, Morocco – you name it, if there was a game to be played and money to be earned we were on the plane. It was that simple.

One of these Keegan trips was fixed up for 16 March, and when I looked at my diary I found it was slap bang in the middle of Cheltenham races, the mecca of horse-racing over the sticks. The trip had been fixed for Dubai in the Middle East, Don Revie's desert refuge after he left the England job. But it was to be Southampton minus Alan Ball. He had criticized Revie severely in a book, so there was some bad feeling btween them and it was requested that he should be left out of the trip. That suited Bally down to the ground. He took the mickey remorselessly, gleefully reminding me that the party didn't get back until Thursday when Cheltenham was well under way.

So I looked at my diary again and said: 'Lawrie, Cheltenham's on three days – Tuesday to Thursday. I've either got the flu or I'm going to Cheltenham!' McMenemy cursed me softly and replied: 'You've obviously got the flu then!' He knew I didn't want to go for the ride, not when the best National Hunt racing in the country was on. He was as good as gold then, but I had let him know exactly what I was doing. I wasn't lying. I could have said I was injured or really had some illness, but I gave him the 'out' to tell me I had got the flu. Southampton went to Dubai and I went to Cheltenham. The whole incident typified the excellent understanding I had with Lawrie.

It was strange the way it worked out when we parted company as manager and player for the last time. One minute I was negotiating a new contract, the next minute I was being shown the door – even though it was on the best of terms.

In my last season at Southampton we were four points clear at the top of the First Division around April time, although the teams below us had two or three games in hand. This was Kevin Keegan's second year with Saints and my third in the second spell. Lawrie agreed that we would sort out my future by the end of the season. The Saints slipped back to fifth and then sixth place, but that was just about our rightful place after the games in hand had been sorted out. I'd had a good season by my own standards, not my best but good enough. Then I got a phone call one afternoon from McMenemy's secretary asking if I would go and see the boss in the morning. I thought at the time it was a bit strange, in fact I remember joking to Alan Ball about it. I said to him it was almost certainly about a new contract, but I'd probably get a free transfer – little did I know that I was right on the button.

I went to see Lawrie, and sure enough he said he thought it was about time we parted company. It shocked me at the time because I thought I'd done well. But with hindsight it was quite understandable. I was earning the best part of £60,000 a year, which would represent the wages of perhaps three players. With the economics of the game starting to turn a bit sour and a lot of clubs finding it hard to balance the books, older players like me were bound to be at risk. McMenemy said that he thought it would be a good time for me to go into management. I didn't argue at the time, but I should have said: 'You must be joking, I can still play for a couple of years. ' When I think back now, saying he thought I should go into management was probably the easy way out for Lawrie – as though he was doing me a favour by giving me a free to release me for a try at a manager's job. But I was never treated less than fairly. I had my contract paid up and I was on my way again.

11 · Travelling into Trouble

I think I was big enough to accept that nothing lasts for ever. Although I may not have liked my sudden departure from The Dell, or agreed with it, that is the sort of situation when you have to pick yourself up and get on with life. It's no good moaning – because nobody listens. Everyone was surprised by Lawrie McMenemy's decision to give me a free transfer, including my old mates Kevin Keegan and Alan Ball. But then the weirdest thing happened. It was near the end of the season when there are a lot of sports dinners and television occasions. Perhaps it was just me, but I suddenly found that people who had been talking to me all my professional life were avoiding me. Whether it was through embarrassment because they couldn't offer me a job I don't know. But if that was the case, then I'm disappointed.

The last thing I wanted was sympathy or a hand-out. I think I'll always be ready to get off my backside and go and do something. It all occurred before the 1982 World Cup in Spain, so I had television work to keep me busy. Then the offer came in to go on the rebel tour of South Africa for very good money. I jumped at it. South Africa was a country I'd been to before and £10,000 for a two-week tour was not to be sneezed at by someone who was without a regular job. As it was, the rebels were only there seven days – and got paid £6,000, a very good week's work.

South Africa is a country I like, although they've obviously got big problems with their politics. I had been there before coaching in the black townships of Soweto and near Durban. I particularly remember playing for Cape Town, a team managed by Frank Lord, who once did the rounds of English clubs as a striker before going into coaching and management. On one occasion we played Kaiser Chiefs, an all-black, star team. They were the Manchester United of Soweto. We had some good players, Johnny Sissons, once of West Ham, and a Young England striker, Mick Hill, who had appeared for Sheffield United and Ipswich back home. Mick was a bit of a bird watcher – the feathered kind I hasten to add.

Football is very big in the black townships. They play soccer all the year round in Soweto. On this particular occasion there was such a big crowd trying to get in, Frank Lord had his team talk interrupted by a request that the kick-off be delayed twenty minutes. Otherwise there might have been a riot.

Eventually we got out on the pitch and the spectators were packed like sardines into a ground that held 35,000. There was wire mesh all around the ground to keep the fans penned in. And they were squeezed in so tightly that the ones closest to the fence had the imprint of the wire pressed into their faces. The air was thick with a blue haze right across the ground – that was the product of some kind of strange tobacco the blacks smoke over there. It's called dakka and I'm told it's a bit like their version of marijuana.

The black players in South Africa have plenty of skill on the ball and they started off by flicking it up and rolling it around their shoulders. The crowd loved and cheered each skilful moment, it made the atmosphere quite electric. If they had got on top they could have caused us problems because of their tremendous skill, but we went ahead after ten minutes when I whipped over a free-kick before everyone else got settled and Mick Hill stuck it away. Before they knew it they were three goals down and we ended up beating them 4–2.

Just before the end you could tell that the fans weren't too pleased, so I waited until we were well on top and I tried a few silly things to amuse the crowd like sitting and kneeling on the ball. All of a sudden we were taking the mickey out of their team after they'd tried to make fools of us early on. The next minute I spotted a bottle coming sailing over the fence and it was going to land quite near me. So I trapped it – as much to protect myself as anything else. That was it, Frank Lord had me off straight away and down to the dressing room before I could try any more antics that might have enraged the crowd.

I remember talking to the owner of the Chiefs, Klaus Kaiser (the team was named after him), and he wanted me to play for them. That was quite an honour, as I would have been the only white man in an all-black team. He lived in a mansion in Soweto, surrounded by all the little huts where all the other people lived. However, they worshipped him. He was a very rich man, king of the castle in that part of the world. I would have loved to have played for him, but it just didn't work out and I had to come back to England to start my second year at Manchester City.

I know that many people believe sportsmen shouldn't go to South Africa because of their apartheid rules, but I was there to work. I'm most definitely opposed to apartheid, but I don't think it would help matters by Mick Channon refusing to go to South Africa, especially as I like to think I helped to encourage the black footballers when I was out there. I had brought pleasure – or misery for those who didn't like me – to whites and blacks alike. I trained barefoot kids in Soweto – and I think that gives me a stronger platform to talk about South Africa than the people who condemn the way things are run there when they haven't been within five thousand miles of the place.

There are a lot of good players in South Africa, and quite a few went into American soccer. One of my Cape Town team mates, a character called 'Jingles' Periera, did join the Kaiser Chiefs and was a bit of star for them. There are any number of huge advertising hoardings and billboards featuring black players endorsing drinks and other commodities – players we've never heard of in Britain.

I have the same repulsion about South Africa's repressive measures as everyone else. I'm not prejudiced in any way and I recognize South Africa has big social problems that the rest of the world just hasn't got. All I know is that you don't find starving black people in South Africa like there are in their millions in Ethiopia, the Sudan and Uganda for instance. That doesn't make apartheid right – but you've got to have a base to work from.

I went to South Africa to work and earn money. If I was wrong, so are British Airways and Lufthansa. They are multi-million-pound companies and there's no pressure on them to stop going to South Africa. I know that two wrongs don't make a right, but I don't believe that isolating South Africa from sport is bringing the political situation any nearer to a solution.

With the rebel tour to South Africa lasting only seven days, Jimmy Hill got in a spot of bother for backing it. Ossie Ardiles and fellow-Argentine World Cup-winner Mario Kempes, plus my old Manchester City and England club mate Dave Watson, all pulled out. Ardiles and Kempes arrived out in Johannesburg, but decided not to go through with the tour. Dave played in the first game, but there was a big stink about him participating so he bowed to the pressure that was coming from the powers that be back home. While I was still out there, I arranged to play with Durban City for a month and by then the season had started back in England.

One of my more light-hearted experiences in South Africa came when I bumped into that legendary former London player Johnny 'Budgie' Byrne. I had played against him when I was a kid and he was a big star. He moved from Crystal Palace to West Ham and was an England regular. He had the kind of skill that made people dub him the British Di Stefano – he was that good. He had been long gone from British football and – as I had thought – had disappeared to the Congo. In fact, he had been in South Africa for a number of years as a player and was then a well-known manager over there. I say that I bumped into him, I couldn't really avoid him because width-wise he was the size of a house! He had always been a little fellow, so his weight gain made him look very large indeed round the middle. But he'd always been known as a character back to his playing days, and he certainly didn't disappoint me on this occasion!

I was over in South Africa playing for Frank Lord's Cape Town City and the other big local club were Hellenic, managed at the time by Budgie Byrne. On the morning of my first game, Frank Lord asked me if I would go and visit Budgie's son who had had a bad accident and was in the heart-transplant hospital, made famous by Christiaan Barnard years ago, the Groote Schuur. I went up to see him and enquired about the chance of seeing his dad. He said he'd seen his father the night before and was told he'd be either at our game or the local race meeting.

I had to laugh because if Budgie had to choose between seeing me play my first game, and a trip to the race track it was no contest – the horses would win by a street! Sure enough he missed the game. Afterwards I took a few of our players back to the hotel and some minutes later who should walk in but Budgie himself. He'd obviously had a cracking day at the races. I don't mean that he'd won because he was renowned as the world's worst betting man, but I'm sure the alcohol he'd consumed had worked very well as an anaesthetic. We got stuck straight into the champagne, but after a short time he said that he couldn't stay because one of his players was getting married and he'd promised to make a speech at the reception. About two hours later, and a half a dozen bottles, he'd decided, or perhaps pleaded was a better description, that I should go with him. That was just the beginning of my troubles as I had a gut feeling that I would be needed for moral support when an irate wife, bridegroom and bride got hold of him.

'I'll need you to apologize to my wife,' was how Budgie put

it. When we arrived at the wedding reception I wasn't far behind him in a state of drunkenness and it was a bit of a job to get up on the stage for the speeches. Budgie just about managed it, then grabbed hold of the microphone, but he was in such a state he could hardly put two words together. He tried to introduce me as well but not too many people could understand what he was saying.

It was no surprise when his attractive wife marched up in front of everyone and gave him some terrible verbal stick for daring to turn up in such a condition. She demanded to know where he'd been and explained angrily that he'd held up the whole party because of his lateness. I'd been given half a volley by the wife as well because Budgie had obviously seen me as an escape from the worst of the wrath, so he'd thrown me the anchor! I suppose his thinking was: 'If I'm going down, I'll take someone with me.' After that Budgie wouldn't leave my side almost as though if he stuck to me he'd escape any more verbal blasting.

Some ten minutes later his wife again rounded on me saying it was all my fault, before dragging poor Budgie off for a dance. The next thing I knew he was flat on the floor, spark out. Whether his wife had hit him or whether it was purely the drink that did it I'm not sure. But it meant I came in for yet more abuse, so I reckoned it was time to make the best of my way out of there. Budgie and I had been drinking from around seven o'clock to nearly ten – but what had he been doing all afternoon? No prizes for that answer!

I'll always love him for being such a warm person. And before I left he came up to me and gave me his autobiography, which I've got at home today. The title was, appropriately enough, *Balls!* Well, he did always like a good time. When I went back to South Africa on the rebel tour two years later he hadn't changed a bit, still a lovable if enormously fat little man.

By this time Budgie wasn't a manager any more but ran a restaurant in Cape Town. I had a virus, but I still insisted on going to see him, and of course he wouldn't let me go. If you were a mate of his, especially someone from England, he'd lock the door. I find people like him precious. He's the kind of character who is sadly missing from the British game these days.

One of my most amazing experiences abroad came directly after I got a free transfer from Southampton. I went out to the Far East to guest for a club in Hong Kong. My offer was to go for just one game, along with a few others from Southampton like David Armstrong and George Lawrence. We were wanted to play for Caroline Hill, a well-known club on the island. It was run by Veronica Chui, a very rich Chinese lady. She owned two teams in the League, and we were wanted to play in the vital last game of the season to prevent one of them from being relegated.

First of all, however, her other team, which were second in the league, had to beat the second-bottom club the night before in order to give Caroline Hill a chance. It should have been a foregone conclusion, and, in fact, only a draw was needed to give our team the chance to save itself the following day.

The owner didn't really need to strengthen her best team, but just to make quite sure of victory, she placed George Lawrence in it – leaving the rest of us to play in the vital game the next day.

George's team were facing a club called South China, who despite their lowly position were the Manchester United of Hong Kong. That alone should have been enough for Madam Chui to smell a rat.

Anyway, horror of horrors, George's team got beaten in the upset of the season. So suddenly our game the following day didn't matter one jot. As it happened we won 2–0, only the third win the team had had for months. The trouble was it was completely meaningless. I felt sorry for the owner, she had gone to all the expense of flying us out to Hong Kong, paid us very good wages to play just the one game – and it had all been for nothing.

Football has been very good to me in that it has allowed me to travel the world. I've been twice to Australia, New Zealand and South Africa, as well as going to Hong Kong, the United States and to many other countries on England and European club trips. Towards the end of my career I've been lucky to go far-away places on my own, to see how football is played by the locals and experience taking part in their game.

In New Zealand I turned out for a club called Blockhouse Bay – probably the worst team I've ever played for when I've been abroad. They were bottom of their league when I went there, and second bottom when I left! And they ended up back at the bottom by the end of their season. Blockhouse would have been village green standard back in England, they were desperate. I then played for a team in New Zealand called Kelston Shantung. They were much better, more like Hampshire County League standard or just below Southern League. I went out there with a character called Sammy Malcolmson, who played in the New Zealand World Cup team. He was originally a Scots lad whom I had known back in my early Southampton days when he was on their books. Sammy had never got very far in British football – playing a few times for Airdrieonians in Scotland – but in New Zealand he's a celebrity with his own sports radio show and sportswear business.

There are some good players in New Zealand, but overall the standard is pretty poor. They just haven't got the level of competition that we have in Britain. There are only three million inhabitants and the good players have never been pushed into improving themselves. When I was out there I suggested that they established liaisons with clubs in Europe and England: places where they could send their players for a winter, during their close season, and then get them back with that extra competitive knowledge. This idea seemed to be well received at the time, but as soon as I got back to England the word filtered through to me that the football establishment in New Zealand thought I should mind my own business and not interfere. I found that attitude strange and disappointing. When I first played in New Zealand we got crowds of 2,000, but figures like that soon dwindled away. For the standard of football that was played, I'm surprised that we got that many at all.

Trevor Brooking was in New Zealand at the same time as me and we provided a nice contrast for the Kiwis. Trevor has always been a bit of a diplomat and I was seen as the rebel. We'd both be guest speakers at dinners. Trevor would be the straight man and I was the villain, telling all the dirty jokes. I fell out with everyone, while they all thought Trevor was the nice guy. Of course, we are two different characters. That is the way Trevor is all the time: he never swears, and only drinks Coke. I was well received while I was there, but as soon as I was gone they couldn't wait to stick the knives into me.

I found that a bit petty, because I think I am the sort of person who can accept open personal criticism. A lot of the brickbats came because I was playing for a very poor side. It doesn't matter how good a player you are, you've still got no chance in a bad team. Going to places such as Blockhouse Bay you have to accept that you must come down to their level. It's no good thinking they can rise to near your standard – if that was the case a significant proportion of New Zealand footballers would be over in England playing.

Despite all the problems, I still enjoyed New Zealand. It's a lovely country with an awful lot to offer. Unfortunately, people there in football are frightened of change, but without it they can never become any kind of force in the game.

Football in Australia is a completely different set-up. Like New Zealand they have got a lot of ex-Brits – many of them rejects from British football who have gone over there and made good lives for themselves. But they also have a lot of Greek, Yugoslav and Italian immigrants to spice up their football. All the different groups want their bit of power and they are very dogged. The Aussies love their sport to be physical – what could be called the 'wham, bam, thank you mam' approach. The only way you'll strike up a decent rapport with an Aussie is to cure him of his inbuilt suspiciousness. They do have this terrible chip on their shoulders about us Poms. I don't see what reason there is for it, and I do have a lot of Aussie mates. Obviously Australia is an attractive place to go for a holiday, but despite going close to reaching the World Cup finals in 1986 I think their game will continue to struggle.

Once again the strength of their game comes down to competition – to improve they must come to Europe and play decent games. There is certainly an awful lot of interest in football in Australia. When the likes of Manchester United and Spurs go there they have to shut the gates, and they get 40,000 crowds for internationals.

On my first trip to Australia I played for a club called Newcastle K.B. Raiders. I went back to them a second time, but it didn't go quite as well. They do have big problems in their leagues because often the different ethnic groups don't get on well together and this leads to the different factions pulling in separate directions. Consequently league football is very disjointed down under.

As always, however, I found some humorous experiences to help me on my way. While playing with Newcastle Raiders I fell in with an Irishman called Chris Doherty, who has been out there since he was a small boy. I couldn't have bumped into a better companion, he was mad on horses and he took me to all the race meetings. I remember driving all the way from Sydney to Brisbane – it takes about eleven hours – for a prestigious 100,000-dollar sprint race. We stayed at the Gold Coast, just outside Brisbane, on the way up, but then it never stopped raining. All the roads were flooded and we stayed the extra day, before driving back on a different inland route. Chris seemed to know about every racehorse in Australia, and one thing I learned is that though the Chinese are supposed to be the biggest gamblers in the world, the Aussies certainly take some beating when it comes to punting. When they put their money on, they've got bags of bottle.

Scotland has been a regular visiting spot on my travels. It may not be too far away, but my receptions up there have been as hostile as any I've encountered in far flung parts. That enmity was inflamed on a Southampton pre-season trip, after England had lost to the Scots 2–1 at Wembley in 1977 (the famous occasion when poor Ray Clemence let the ball through his legs to give Scotland their decisive goal). The likes of Peter Osgood, Jimmy McCalliog and Jim Steel were on this particular Saints trip, so fun and games were guaranteed.

We were up in Scotland at Ibrox Park, the Rangers ground, to play in a long-forgotten competition called the Caledonian Trophy. Manchester City, the club I was to join later, were also in it. Southampton played City, drew and even after every player on both sides had taken penalties the scores were still level. We ended up going through the spin of a coin. Two nights later we were due to play Rangers.

Being an England regular at that time I was a natural target for reporters north of the border, especially if they wanted something controversial about Anglo-Scottish football relations. There was a lot of bad feeling around at that time, particularly after Clem's howler against Scotland followed by Press reports that I had taken the defeat especially hard. I had thrown my boots across the dressing room and snapped: 'Those bastards are out there doing a lap of honour.' I don't know how that got out, but it was reported in the papers. Not surprisingly it was rumoured that I hate the Scots – quite rightly, I may add! But only in a football sense, of course.

Therefore it was no surprise that I took an awful lot of stick from the crowd in that first match. We were staying at Stirling in the big university complex there. A female reporter, from one of the Scottish papers, came from Glasgow to interview me. She asked me about the bad feeling and inquired as to what I thought was the best thing about Scotland. I couldn't resist it and, as a joke, replied: 'The road to England.' Then she asked if it was right that I hated

Glasgow. Yes, I said, I hated parts of Glasgow like I hate parts of Southampton, London or Liverpool. We were due to play Rangers the next night and the crowd was really fired up, having read in the paper: 'Channon hates Scotland. The best thing about it is the road to England. He hates Glasgow.' Oddly enough, just to enrage the locals a bit more, I scored after about four minutes. But they had the last laugh because two minutes later I pulled a hamstring and had to go off.

The next day I was booked on a flight to go home. That was very unfortunate for me because a few of us had arranged a coach that day to go from Stirling to Ayr races. You can guess the only four who wanted to go: me, Ossie, Jimmy Mac and Steeley! But with the new League season coming up in about ten days time I had to go back south to get fit. I was to learn later that the coach left Stirling at ten o'clock in the morning, and went via the great Jim Baxter's pub in Glasgow.

Baxter was one of the all-time greats as a Scotland player and his pub was a well-known watering hole, especially for football folk up from England. Of course, in his day, Baxter was also a legendary figure in the annals of drinking footballers. I'm sure he made our lads feel very much at home, and they certainly didn't need to be dragged to any bar. Not surprisingly the coach trip to Ayr races never did get any further than Baxter's pub. It was turned straight round that night and sent back to Stirling. I certainly missed a very good expedition there! I was probably the only one of the four who would have been odds-on to make sure the coach did get to the racetrack, although I would have encountered powerful opposition. I liked a drink as much as anyone, but the horses would always come first for me.

12 · Kevin Keegan

Kevin Keegan and I go all the way back to being England rookies together when first called up by Sir Alf Ramsey. Since then I've been as close as any other player to Kevin and, of course, we had a marvellous time together as club mates at Southampton when I had my second spell down there. With Alan Ball we made up the South Coast's answer to the Three Musketeers. We went everywhere together, even when we weren't playing. If there was a horse to back, a race to see or a good lads' day out to be had, we were on our way. If we happened to be on a foreign visit, and there were plenty of those while Kevin was with Saints, we'd be off and running.

I like to think I've got as much idea about what makes Kevin tick as anybody in the game. He's not the easiest person to get to know, although through the media he comes across quite brilliantly to the public as everyone's favourite football hero. You won't hear any dirt dished about the fellow, he has managed his public life superbly and if he's a millionaire he has earned every penny of his money. But at least I can let people into a few secrets about the private man that I hope will give some indication as to what drives him as a person, and also how he likes to enjoy life.

To get the serious bit over first, I've no doubts at all on two counts. He reached his peak as a professional player not as a European Player of the Year at Hamburg or as a European Cup-winner at Liverpool but in his second year at

Southampton. Secondly he quit the game absurdly early when he still had so much to give.

In that second season at Southampton, and running on to his move to Newcastle, he was right at the very top, at the height of his powers. He only went to Newcastle because of his Mr Southampton personality-clash with Lawrie McMenemy, as I have already documented. Newcastle was simply another challenge, his playing standards certainly hadn't dropped at all. Challenges have always given him his kicks. Without them, he would never have been the player he was. He took Newcastle by storm. When I went up to Tyneside for a brief stay as a player his name was on everyone's lips. I know the Geordie supporters have always had a great reputation for getting behind their teams, but it was Keegan who galvanized them into becoming such fantastic followers of the team in modern times. He brought out their passion and fervour better than anyone else could have done.

Amazingly, that was the time when Bobby Robson, just starting to flex his muscles as England manager, decided to leave Kevin out of his team – a decision that I found incredibly short-sighted. On reflection, Robson was trying to be shrewd and show early on that he had the strength to say: 'I'm bigger than Kevin Keegan.' Bobby Robson wanted to make a big impression as team manager and he couldn't make a more forceful move than to discard Kevin Keegan. At that time Kevin was by far the best player in the country, and it would be strange to suggest that Kevin didn't deserve his England place on merit.

I may have had many a row down the years over it, but my old maxim always will be: pick your best and strongest team, no matter what the circumstances. This is something which Robson failed to do by jettisoning Kevin, and in my view it did the England manager no credit at all. I am also convinced that Robson's decision had something to do with Kevin eventually retiring as early as he did. Bobby Robson killed a little part of the burning light that drove Keegan on, the day Kevin was dropped by England. He just didn't have the incentive to continue to play at no higher than club level.

I used to travel into Newcastle with Kevin to go training, so I knew how upset he was when England no longer wanted him. I was disappointed that Robson didn't just pick up the phone and tell Kevin: 'Look, I'm going to leave you out. I'm not going to play you.' Kevin felt he was hard done by, although I pointed out to him that when I was dropped no phone call or letter was forthcoming either. I remember saying to Kevin: 'Just forget it, leave it. They've got to have you back because there's no one better.' But by then Kevin had made up his own mind that that was the end of his England career. He simply said to me that he'd never play for England again. It was certainly Kevin's loss – but it was a far bigger loss to England. Surely there's no doubt about it, at that time Kevin's knowledge, ability and super fitness still left him way in front of any pretenders to his crown as the best player in English football.

I can also pinpoint the game when I became aware that Kevin had made up his mind to retire completely from first-class football. I had moved on from my brief spell with Newcastle and had settled in at Norwich. I talked to him towards the end of the season, in the aftermath of the live televised FA Cup-tie between Liverpool and Newcastle. We chatted afterwards and *that* was the game which made him decide to turn it in. He said to me that he couldn't go on. I recall he talked about an incident involving him and Mark Lawrenson from the game. He had gone on a run only to find Lawrenson a bit quicker than him. For Kevin it was time to call it a day. Yet over a longish distance of ground there were several around who were quicker than him. He just compensated by becoming a lot cuter. The years had been good to him and he had certainly lost none of his effectiveness.

Even now I still tell Kevin that he retired with two or three great years to come. He would have gone back in the First Division with Newcastle, the whole area idolized him and the club had a few better players to help him. His know-how was greater then than it had ever been. He'd become a wily old fox. His speed, or lack of it, didn't matter because he was still so sharp over five to ten yards – and that's where it counts in the highest class. Of course, he was going to get in isolated situations, having to go on the occasional run where he was going to be shown up. But you are a lot more astute at thirty than you can ever be in your early twenties and Kevin could have steamed on.

The trouble with Kevin is that he dreaded going downhill as a player. He hated the thought of ending up as a shadow of his former self. He wanted to get out at the top and he certainly did. There's no going back with Kevin Keegan once he's made his mind up. Once he's decided to do something, he's very single-minded and goes ahead and does it.

Kevin won't miss playing the game. He'll simply set himself another challenge in life, whether it be riding in the Grand National – he'll break his neck if he tries! – or getting his golf handicap down. He'll practise his golf until he reaches a very high standard, because that's the way he does things. He likes coaching kids at football, and this takes him all over the world. He'll always have something to do.

I'm sure Kevin has made more money than any other player out of the game. He's a great example to any young player on how to manage oneself. He's brilliant on the public relations side, and he would work hard at every aspect of his life to get it right. He would give his heart and soul to make any project that he tackled succeed. We are still good mates, even though we did end up owning a few horses that were a bit useless! Well, he's still a friend of mine – but I don't know whether I'm a friend of his after some of the horses and tips I've given him.

Kevin perfected the art of capturing the public's imagination. His all-action, all-effort, power-packed way of playing the game, his enthusiasm, work-rate and even his lack of height made him the people's hero. He gave hope to every little guy. When he was simply the best in the business, during that terrific year at Southampton, we just used to load the gun and he would fire the bullets. He was absolutely outstanding. It was the last season for both of us at Southampton, and I especially remember his brilliance when we beat Manchester United 3–2 at The Dell. That day he 'scored' with an amazing overhead kick, only to see it ruled out by the referee for offside. He'd hooked a shot over his head and it flew into the top corner of the net with nobody possibly interfering with play. Unfortunately, my good self had wandered into a position that was technically off-side so, in fact, I ruined what should have been the goal of the season. I think I was leaning on the corner flag at the time, getting my breath back! I was just lucky enough to have played with Kevin when he was at his best.

Why was Kevin Keegan an even greater player with Saints than he had been at Hamburg or Liverpool? The answer is possibly because he had to carry Southampton more as a team. He was of greater importance to Southampton than he could have been at Liverpool or Hamburg. I think I'm in a good position to make a judgement because even when he was at Anfield and in West Germany I was still a regular team mate of his in the England side so I could keep a first-hand impression of his form.

Kevin may be well off now, but I remember a day when he, Alan Ball and myself were left without a bean.

In the Keegan days at Southampton, players needed almost to have a permanently-packed suitcase and their passports were peppered with entry and departure stamps. I certainly enjoyed going to exciting places like Malaysia and the United States: and it was in America that we once ended up stony-broke. Yes, you've guessed it, after a day at the races – and I was highly unpopular with the lads.

We were in the States for a big tournament, flying into Seattle first. Lawrie McMenemy hadn't come with us and John Mortimore, who had been at the club during my first spell, was back as No. 2 and in charge of this trip. We were in the States for ten days and given spending money of around £100. We arrived jet-lagged and after a night out we went and played golf. By then Kevin, Alan and I had hardly any money between us. We were like Athos, Porthos and Aramis knocking around together, and on the second day we were going racing.

The three of us were contemplating what was left of our spending money, as we demolished a few beers. Showing what a truly international superstar Kevin was by this time, loads of people spotted him while hardly anybody recognized Bally, even though he'd won the Soccer Superbowl with Vancouver the previous season. One of the fellows who had recognized Kevin gave him a tip for a horse.

We pooled all our money and I went up to the Tote to put it on. The Musketeers went back to the track-side and roared this animal home. It won by around twenty lengths and up at the Tote it was showing about 5–2. We'd had about 200 dollars on, all the money that we had left. I went up to cash in the ticket. It went into the machine and came out as a losing ticket. I hadn't checked the numbers on the ticket when I had put the bet on – and it was the hardest lesson of my life. Either I had been given the wrong number or I might have given the Tote people the wrong one – but whatever the mistake, it added up to a big, fat zero result. I remember going back to Kevin and Bally and they couldn't believe it.

Now we were skint, and John Mortimore couldn't help us out because he didn't have a bean. Lawrie was meeting us over in New York, after having been down to his house in Florida. So the only thing left to get us out of trouble was the old stand-by, the American Express card. I remember Bally coming up to me back home after the trip and saying: 'Have you received your American Express bill yet?' I said no and asked him how much his came to. He replied: 'A Jumbo.' I said: 'A Jumbo – what do you mean?' 'You know,' retorted Bally, 'a 747 – seven hundred and forty-seven quid!' I quipped that I probably hadn't got my bill because my American Express card had melted under the strain. That was a very good trip.

The Three Musketeers

When Don Revie was in charge of England, he was the first manager to assemble the squad for week-long get-togethers. However, that didn't stop Kevin and I from breaking camp to follow our second love, horse-racing.

Revie had taken the England lads to the Hungerford Hydro, just outside Newbury. It was a health farm. Being locked up in one of those places meant just one thing – boredom. The week-long session was made possible by one weekend's fixtures being put off to enable the England manager to have an uninterrupted week with his players. There was almost nothing to do, and you can imagine that with a team of footballers locked away it was driving many of us up the wall.

By the Thursday I'd almost had enough, and after we'd finished our training in the morning I suggested to Kevin that we break camp and take off for Devon and Exeter races. John Baker, one of the trainers I have horses with, had two running that day – Lucky Victory and Nan's Gem. I said to Kevin: 'Look, we're almost on the M4 here. I'll get my mate to come down and run us down there.' My pal had a Jensen Interceptor, a powerful car that was just the job for a high-speed dash to Devon and Exeter and back.

We were duly picked up, hit the motorway and roared down to the Devon and Exeter meeting. It was well over a hundred miles, but we hammered it on to the M5, past Bristol and then Taunton, to Exeter and straight on to the racecourse.

A lot of people knew me as a regular racegoer, but at that time Kevin Keegan was still something of a rare sight at the tracks. To our horror, no sooner were we there than the cameras started clicking and the word went round that these two England players, who were supposed to be locked up in a health hydro, were having a day at the races.

Both John Baker's horses won and we backed the second of them at 8–1. We shot back up the motorways and got back to Hungerford, just half-an-hour late for tea around half past six. Revie had a bit of a long face but seemingly we had got away with our little escapade at 'playing truant'.

Kevin and I didn't do anything that evening, but the following morning we woke up to a phone call from Kevin's wife, Jean, giving him a right rollicking. She had gone down to her in-laws in the West Country, in the Newquay area, had picked up the local paper – and there was a picture of Kevin and me on the steps of the racecourse complete with binoculars! She said: 'I thought you were away training with England and I pick up the paper to find you were at Devon and Exeter.' Kevin was definitely a bit red-faced over that escapade.

With Lawrie McMenemy and Kevin Keegan around there's no doubt that we always did things in style at Southampton. We were always guaranteed to go to impressive places and have a good time. One such hilarious outing came when we were doing particularly well in the First Division, during Kevin's second year at The Dell. There had been an exhibition put on at the Brighton Conference Centre, and to round it off McMenemy had fixed up a five-a-side match with Brighton to be played at eight o'clock in the evening. This was another occasion when football nearly got in the way of my racing interests: the meeting that day was at nearby Plumpton. But as we had been in such good form in the League Lawrie thought he'd reward us with a day at the races, and then we could go on to the Conference Centre for the five-a-side match.

The Three Musketeers were in their element, going to the races along with Lawrie plus coach Lew Chatterley. Lawrie had arranged for us to get in the members' enclosure and we'd had an excellent lunch. It was a smashing day out at a nice little racetrack. I'll never forget Lawrie approaching me and Bally, the so-called experts, before the first couple of races asking us what we'd fancied. We gave him short-priced tips and he'd had his couple of quid on only to see them both get beaten. So he said to us: 'Away you lads. I'm picking out a horse for myself in the next race.' Being a Geordie he went for something with the Tyne in its name.

Lawrie had a quid on at around 25–1, and it only bolted home in a modest hunter chase! That was it, we couldn't keep him quiet for the rest of the afternoon. It was that kind of fun day. We'd had a great time and plenty to drink as well. Lawrie and Lew went back to the hotel – no rubbish, the Imperial, when Lawrie did something he did it in style. The rest of the team had stayed at the hotel while we were racing and knocking back champagne. Bally and Kevin were in my car while the boss and Lew had gone in Lawrie's car. At the races we met somebody who had a pub in Brighton so Bally, Kevin and me, having had a few drinks, shot back there to carry on our enjoyment. With us having a drink there was a fifty-year-old, peroxide blond with a green streak in her hair who had been at the races. She must have been about fourteen stone and was well known for being a local character. In our jolly state somebody bet Keegan £100 for charity that he couldn't carry this old dear on his shoulders from the pub to another boozer about half a mile away. We all had a whip-round in the pub for £100 – it was never a good thing to offer Kevin a bet on anything because he wouldn't let anything beat him. Sure enough he picked up the lady and raced up a quite steep hill for half a mile – round the other pub and back to the starting point. It was a hilarious sight to see Britain's most famous footballer haring along a quiet street in Brighton with an old dear on his back, Alan Ball chasing along behind as the referee and the old lady's face going the colour of the green streak in her hair. But he won his bet and picked up the £100 – for charity. The piggy-back ride must have hurt the old girl more than it did Kevin because he was always a strong little devil for his size.

Eventually we got down to the Conference Centre where Lew Chatterley had laid the kit out and one of our players, Nick Holmes, who likes to do everything just right, was waiting. Kevin, Bally and myself had all had our fair share of drink, but Kevin was the lucky one because he was put in goal. Bally and I had to the exhausting work out on the pitch with a skinful of drink inside us!

The fourteen-stone challenge

It was a cracking five-a-side and good for us because we needed a sweat. We got beaten 5–4 in the end and although it was an exhibition game the old, professional competitive spirit came out and tempers flared. So much so that Neil McNab – that fiery little Scot, who was playing for Brighton at that time – butted Bally in the face. But it was McNab who came off worst because he split his head open by catching Bally's teeth! There was a big fuss in the papers about it and they both got hauled in front of a disciplinary committee over the incident. Still, we weren't going to let it spoil the enjoyment of a great day out and we ended up in a casino called Sergeant Pepper's and had a good dinner as well. It had been another good day out with Lawrie McMenemy and the Southampton smart set, and another insight to the character and terrific spirit of Kevin Keegan. He's badly missed in the game.

13 · In the Wilderness

Looking back on the last few fabulous years at Norwich and then Portsmouth, chasing trophies with both clubs, it's hard to believe the problems I had to find a settled football home after getting a free from Southampton.

Anyone would have thought I was all washed-up, with unsatisfactory spells at Newcastle and Bristol Rovers behind me. Perish the thought, but I was even starting to feel sorry for myself until I got a rude awakening from Peter Shilton. It was really down to Peter that, as the song goes, I shook myself off, dusted myself down – and started all over again. When I had got back to England after another bit of globe-trotting to Hong Kong and South Africa, it looked as though there was nothing for me after Southampton. Whether clubs were frightened of me because of my outspoken views on television or perhaps they thought I'd want too much money, I don't know. All I can say is that nobody asked me to do a job for them and it looked as though I was right out on my ear. However, there was just a glimmer of hope, thanks to my old mate Kevin Keegan. He'd moved from Southampton to Newcastle, and suddenly I got a call suggesting that I ring Newcastle manager, Arthur Cox. To this day – and I still don't really know if it's true – I'm sure that it was down to Kevin, who had gone up there to help a once great club back into the big time again. Anyway, it led to me going to the north-east as well, two weeks into the season, and trying my luck.

It was obvious to me right from the start that Newcastle weren't going to go up to the First Division in Kevin's first year. They had a load of promising kids who were very keen but the club wasn't good enough, at that stage, to go up. I scored in my first game, against Middlesbrough, but then we struggled and got beaten quite convincingly by Barnsley at home. I knew then we had a few problems.

Newcastle went to Shrewsbury and played extremely well, but amateurish mistakes meant we lost 2–1 after going into the lead. I blew my top in the dressing room afterwards, because all the good work had been thrown away.

It was then that I realized it wasn't going to work for me at Newcastle. Kevin Keegan had been talking to me and I knew the black and whites were splashing out on more new players, buying Terry McDermott and getting David McCreery back from America. So it couldn't work for me. Arthur Cox gave me a call, I had a chat with him and I was on the plane back south the next morning, my Newcastle adventure over.

I did start to think that perhaps there was nothing for me in England any more. I got a call from my old Southampton team mate, the original 'Ale House' player John McGrath, who by then was manager of Port Vale. John was a good, honest lad and I wanted to see if I could help him out. Bobby Gould, who was managing Bristol Rovers, also got in touch. I didn't know what to do because I still didn't want to give the game up.

I thought I'd visit the two clubs straightaway: it was the least I could do if they had had the courtesy to ask me to play for them. I had a good chat with Big Jake McGrath, and in typical form he told me a few good jokes and stories. I could see that Vale had been a useful side and it was a lovely ground, but I just couldn't see it working out with me so far away from my home base.

Bobby Gould put up a very good case down at Bristol. He thought Rovers could get promotion from the Third Division and I agreed to go there on a part-time basis, training just

A haunted figure at Maine Road in 1977.

Helping out Bobby Gould at Bristol Rovers.

(*Opposite*) I had a new lease of life at Carrow Road and was determined to do well on the 'Village Green'.

CUP FINAL
1985

The Norwich team celebrate winning the 1985 Milk Cup final.

Cheers, Asa!

It was magic to get my son on to the Wembley turf, and I've got Ken Brown to thank for the privilege.

Jamesmead – my best horse yet.

(*Left*) Heading my second goal against Wimbledon, during a Division Two encounter in 1986.

(*Below*) The goalscorer receives the congratulations of his team mates.

Still enjoying the game after more than twenty years at the top.

one day a week. That was a mistake from the very beginning.

If there was one thing I was to learn in the game, it was that to play professional football you have to give more than one day a week in preparation. I was delighted that Bobby offered me the chance, but it was more of a public relations exercise for the Rovers manager to push the name of the club in the city. He'd got an experienced England player to go and sign on for Bristol Rovers, which was quite a coup for a strictly small-time club. As it turned out I had only a handful of games for them in the couple of months leading up to Christmas-time.

That's where Peter Shilton came in. Our careers probably started at a similar time, me at Southampton and Peter at Leicester. I recall seeing him for the first time, up at Lilleshall, and thinking what a big lad he was. Even as a kid he was a giant, and an absolute fanatic about his training and his goalkeeping. Perhaps that dedication explained why he became one of the great keepers in the world. I've known him down the years as an England colleague, but we missed being club mates at Southampton.

It was while my career was dwindling away at Bristol Rovers as a part-timer that I had a day out racing at Fontwell with Alan Ball. Shilts was racing mad as well and sure enough he was there. We had a very pleasant afternoon, laced with more than a few drinks. Southampton were having a bit of a bad time then; Shilts had just arrived and Bally was on his way to Hong Kong as a player. It was the same old story, we did our dough and ended up in a restaurant, licking our betting wounds.

A fair amount of drink had been taken on board and the tongues were loosened. I told Shilts what a bore he was and that he was only interested in getting people behind the ball, not in playing the game entertainingly. Peter retorted by saying what a great manager he would be when he finished playing. (He really believes he will end up as manager of England: he has a tremendous self-confidence about him.) Here was I, nearly retired, and then Peter had a go at me. He called me a lazy so-and-so and told me I should get off my backside and get training every day. He said that if anyone ought to know it was him that you can't play the game at a decent level without putting in the training every day.

I certainly sat up and took notice of this stinging criticism. I owe him a lot for that: and once I got the opportunity to play at Norwich and manager Ken Brown asked if I wanted to be a part-timer, I said no. I wanted to go to Norwich and give it a good crack, full time. Consequently I've lasted a good few years more than I expected.

Peter and I have always had our arguments. Shilts would certainly be in my original team of moaners: he's never happy. But there again I'd probably get picked for it as well and we'd be team mates!

Nothing gives me greater pleasure in the game than to stuff Peter Shilton, and I'm sure he feels exactly the same thing about me. But we've always managed to be civil to each other and buy each other a drink, especially at the races. There is certainly no grudge between us. It's just that we've been together so much on England trips and he's the most boring card player I've ever met in my life! Some people used to call him Mogadon, after the sleeping tablet, because he could make everyone nod off, he was that long making a decision on which card to play.

During my last season with Norwich, I got a lot of stick for going in late and high on Peter in a match against Southampton. The ball came over my shoulder; I was trying to watch the bounce; and then stuck my foot out. The top of Peter's thigh and his stomach seemed to get in the way. He needed a lot of attention before be could carry on, but to this day I maintain he made too much of it. I'm not considered to be a rough, tough, old-style battering ram of a striker. But people forget that I've always gone in hard on goalkeepers if I've thought there was a chance of nicking the ball. You don't score more than 300 goals in a career without making

'Never play cards with Shilts . . .'

a few enemies of the men who stand between the posts.

Goalkeepers are too much of a protected species, especially by referees. If they go for a ball and drop it, landing on their backside, it always seems to end with a free-kick awarded to them. Keepers, in my opinion, are the most boring people in the game: great off the pitch maybe, but on it they get up my nose. They are in a world of their own.

Shilts missed the next game, but I'll always remember that my old boss Lawrie McMenemy had no complaints about my challenge. Norwich had beaten them 1–0, and in the middle of the following week I bumped into Lawrie before watching a Southampton game at The Dell. He said: 'Your mate's not too pleased with you. He can't play tonight. He's got a dead leg and a bad thigh.' I replied: 'Lawrie, there's only one thing I can say. If I had been playing for you I would have done exactly the same.' He simply said: 'I know you would have.' He had no complaints, though.

I don't think a dead leg ever stopped me, although I suppose a goalkeeper has to stand around and can't get it warmed up sufficiently like an outfield player. Shilts complained about those stud marks for a long time. I don't know why because I told him I'd sign them! The referee certainly didn't think my challenge had been a bad one because I wasn't booked.

It was the day before Christmas Eve during my Bristol Rovers spell and I was at home tending my horses when Bobby Gould rang and said: 'Do you fancy having a crack at the First Division again?' I couldn't get in my car quickly enough, even though it was a 190-mile trek to the club where I was to spend some of the happiest days of my life. . . Norwich City.

That call came just in time because I was seriously considering packing the game in. I wasn't fit, I was overweight and I wasn't training nearly enough – I couldn't have gone on like that. The weight addition wasn't serious, but the pounds will pile on if you are suddenly reduced to just one day's training a week and playing once every two weeks. You can't get away with that in professional football.

I had to give Norwich manager Ken Brown a ring, and he asked if I could get up there by the following morning, Christmas Eve. That was a problem because I'd had a crash in my own car, so I had to hire a Mini. The space was a bit cramped for a biggish lad like me to go on a long drive all the way to Norwich. And the journey included a laborious haul along the A11 before they'd built the motorway that goes out to East Anglia through Essex. It seemed to take forever, what with all the Christmas traffic as well – but who cared? I'd just been given the best Christmas present of my life.

Initially my assignment was only for a month. All I knew was that I had nothing to lose by giving it a go back on the stage I loved the best – the English First Division. Ken Brown asked me whether I wanted to work part-time and I realized then, after my experiences with Bristol Rovers, that I had to approach this job with a far more professional attitude. Norwich were bottom of the First Division and I was needed to play on Boxing Day because strikers John Deehan and Keith Bertschin were out through injury and suspension. And coming up on Boxing Day was the big East Anglian derby at Ipswich. That was some début for me and we won 3–2. I didn't score, but it was the best start possible for me. On the next day we played Luton. We won 1–0 and I got the winner. It was perfect.

I'll never forget that first day at Norwich when Ken Brown took me through to meet the chairman, Sir Arthur South. Ken said to me: 'If it wasn't for the chairman, you wouldn't be here. It was him who suggested you.' So it's thanks to Sir Arthur that I had two and a half sweet years at Norwich.

Sir Arthur South was a great old character, in many ways like my chairman at Southampton for so many years, George Reader. They were from the old school of chairmen. It made Sir Arthur's day when Norwich won at Wembley, and when I went up the famous stairs to collect the Milk Cup I could see a tear in his eyes. He was crying, bless him. George Reader was much the same when Southampton had lifted the FA Cup those years before.

Back in that first season with Norwich we ended up getting out of trouble and finishing near halfway in the First Division table. I had two more seasons there, culminating in that Milk Cup win. I was on a month-to-month contract all the way through. I simply didn't want to be stuck at Norwich if I wasn't playing in the side and things weren't going well. With a month-to-month deal we could part company quickly on the best of terms.

I had found out, later on in my life, that freedom was more important than the security. You can do what you want, go where you want and be your own boss. I'm not saying that I'm so financially secure that I don't need money. But the freedom to do what I want helps me to do my job well. I can give it my best shot, and if it doesn't work I can move on without being a burden to anyone. That way I'm not costing anyone money. I'm not getting bored and fed up with no pleasure in life. If I am getting pleasure then I know I'm doing a good job.

So from having nearly retired at Christmas – one step away from the scrap-heap – I had found a happy, new football home where life was going to get even better. That is the fascinating part fate plays in a footballer's life – who knows where the game will lead us? After everything that has happened to me, I wouldn't care to predict my next move.

14 · On the Village Green

To get the call from Norwich City and eventually help them to their first major trophy was like a dream come true. But that dream could so easily have been shattered by the man whose coaching methods I have respected more than anybody else's during my whole career.

They were two and a half lovely years at Carrow Road. Norwich suited me and I suited Norwich. But my outspoken ways and lifelong refusal to keep quiet when I believe something has to be said nearly got me the sack.

I had an excellent relationship with the crowd at Carrow Road. Ken Brown, the manager, was great to me. He was the one who took me on – even though it was the chairman, Sir Arthur South, who first mentioned my name. But I always felt that Ken didn't really trust me, even that deep down he didn't actually want me. It may be a strange thing to say, but I always got the feeling that he wanted to get rid of me, as if I was some sort of threat to him. Nothing was said. It was just a feeling that I had, but sometimes I wondered if Ken thought I was getting too popular at Norwich. Yet after saying that, I must state that Ken Brown was and is perfect for Norwich as a fine front man.

There's no doubt about it, in my opinion, most of the brains and the hard work on the footballing side come from the coach, Mel Machin. Mel's the best I've played under, and if I ever owned a club or was a manager I wouldn't hesitate to offer a job to Mel. That doesn't mean to say I

Happy days at Norwich

didn't have my disagreements with him. And one big bust-up before a game led to him revealing to me later that he had thought very seriously about asking to get me fired from Norwich. That doesn't bear thinking about when I think of what we went on to achieve together. It would have been very sad if we'd parted before we'd really got to know what each other was like.

The incident occurred during my second season at Norwich when we had a very bad result in the FA Cup. I had completed half a season in my first year, helping the club off the bottom of the First Division to safety. In the following season we went to Derby County in the FA Cup and got knocked out. We were unlucky in lots of ways. The referee gave a diabolical penalty decision against us and we went down 2–1. At the time Derby were a struggling Second Division team and on the slippery slope downwards so it was a bad result for us. Derby had lots of experience and they gave the ball bags of welly. John Robertson, their tricky, little Scotland winger, conned the referee rotten to get a penalty by diving in the box. He had plenty of form for that stroke. After that it was always an uphill battle and we lost out. Mel Machin was very much the disciplinarian at Norwich and we could tell he was in a bad mood all week over the Derby defeat.

Mel was the solid, stable man in the partnership with manager Ken Brown. Mel was the one who kicked backsides, while Ken was the nice guy. Ken is great at the organizing side. He's very enthusiastic and wants to play attacking football and that suited me. Mel and Ken were a great combination.

Mel had obviously bottled up his feelings all week, and he bided his time until he gave us the dressing-room talk on the Saturday before we went out to face West Ham United at home. He was in a blazing mood and it all poured out that afternoon.

Mel started off by saying the supporters had said the players had let them down. This was three-quarters of an hour before we were due to play West Ham. I blew my top. I said that there was no way we'd let anybody down for lack of effort, even though the side had played badly on the day. There was a massive, stand-up row. We were calling each other names, and even Ken Brown couldn't stop it. The younger lads had never seen anything like it. But one of the reasons I did it was because we had been going so well I didn't want everything to fall apart through one bad result at Derby. We managed to calm down. Then we went out and beat West Ham 1–0, playing well into the bargain. Yet at the end when we came in I could see that Mel was still sulking, even though he was delighted to have won.

I used to shoot off straight after the games in order to get back home, and unless there was a midweek game I would have a long weekend before driving back to Norwich. So it wasn't until the middle of the following week that I saw Mel again. It was then he told me that he had been shaking all weekend. He said: 'I was so mad and upset.' I said to him, what I've said to countless others in my career, that it wasn't a personal attack on him. It was a reflection of my desire for Norwich to do well. I just wanted all the lads to be right on that day. Yes, it was a bad result at Derby but that had gone. It was then he told me: 'I wanted to sack you there and then for that.' But eventually I think Mel came round to my way of thinking. Admittedly we'd had a blazing row – but we always had a lot of healthy respect for each other. We both benefited from that confrontation.

When Norwich did go on to win the Milk Cup the following season Mel said he thought I should go and get a manager's job. But I'd heard similar words a couple of years earlier from Lawrie McMenemy. I told Mel I thought I was still good to carry on playing for a bit. I didn't always agree with Mel, but for me his organization, his defensive set-ups, his free-kicks and set plays made him second to none as a coach. His training sessions were great, always very interesting so the players didn't get bored. It was hard training, possibly the hardest I've ever experienced in my club career.

Mind you, I wasn't averse to taking a few short cuts by this stage in my career – and I think Mel used to make certain allowances for me and Asa Hartford, my old Manchester City running mate, who had joined me again at Norwich.

I always got on well with Ken Brown, but I felt he was bad at making decisions. His indecision was final, as they say.

Whether Ken had problems with the board I don't know, but I do know that players sometimes had difficulty tying him down to decisions over things like contracts. Mine was straight-forward, being a monthly agreement, but I found it hard at the end of a season to get him to say whether he wanted me again. He'd tell me not to worry, that we'd work it out when I got back from one of my close-season trips abroad. I just couldn't get hold of him at the times when I thought he should have sorted things out.

Ken could also be somewhat indecisive in his team selection. He could be very jittery, and in my view made the biggest rick of his managerial career in the Milk Cup semi-final, first leg at Ipswich – only to get away with it. He had been edgy for days, and then decided to play a young, inexperienced midfield lad called Paul Clayton, who we used to call 'Clanger'. It nearly was too.

Paul was a lad who had come through the youth team. (To be fair to Norwich they do give the young players a chance.) But this crucial semi-final away leg was not the game to give him that opportunity. Ken had left Louie Donowa out. Louie is a player who I've certainly criticized in the past, but he would have caused more problems to Ipswich than Clayton could. Sure enough, in the first-half Ipswich murdered us. I partly blamed myself for Ipswich's goal. I was at the far post when Mich D'Avray pinched half a yard on me and got in a great header that flew into the corner of our net.

We didn't kick a ball in the first half. We played atrociously and should have been two or three down. When we came in at half-time Ken Brown's West Ham background came to the fore. All he wanted us to do was play; to knock the ball around – that's great . . . in the right circumstances. Ken would have his say and get his point over. But I said: 'Just a minute, we're losing 1–0. The first thing we mustn't do is give any more goals away. If it's got to be 1–0, let's keep it at 1–0. It doesn't matter how we are playing.'

Ken Brown went very quiet. He had wanted us to go out and play and beat them on the day. But sometimes in football you can't do that. When you're playing badly, you can't just pick it up, especially when there is a home leg to come. So as we went out on the pitch for the second-half I said to the lads: 'Let's keep it tight.' I love to get forward and entertain as much as anyone, and if we had been in good nick I would have been the first to encourage us to give it a go. But we weren't getting a kick. Again, it wasn't through lack of effort, it was just that on the day we didn't play. That we managed to keep it at 1–0, considering our poor form, was quite a feat. We were close to reaching the biggest day of our lives, collectively as a team, so we scraped and battled to hold on for a 1–0 defeat. In the second leg we came out and performed well, won 2–0 and we were at Wembley.

If we'd lost it badly in the first leg I would have blamed Ken Brown for his selection of Paul Clayton, just when we needed to keep it tight. Obviously Ken rated the lad, but I didn't. He was just a youth – a boy expected to do a man's job on the night. However, we did survive and went through to a memorable day in my life – and one that my family will never forget.

Norwich have this lovely policy that everyone at the football club matters, from the dressing-room cleaner to the best players. And as far as Sir Arthur South was concerned, that feeling spread outside the club. I recall going up to London with Sir Arthur on the train at the time he was leading the League's television negotiating committee. He was telling me that every club in the League would get £30,000. He said to me: 'I think it's a good deal.' I saw him the next week after the intervention of club chairmen Robert Maxwell, Ken

Bates and Irving Scholar and their insistence that they could do better. They said there was a far better deal to be negotiated – and look what happened. Everyone ended up getting far less and perhaps Swansea, who went bankrupt, might have been saved that hardship by the £30,000 that was originally on offer. Sir Arthur knew that the original deal would benefit those that needed it most.

It was sad for me to see Sir Arthur having to step down from the Norwich board over the rebuilding of the new stand. I'm sure it was something that caused him a lot of heartache, although I'm a great believer that the club is bigger than any individual and life must go on. I'll treasure the memories of Sir Arthur coming in our dressing room before games and sitting down next to me for a laugh and a joke. People like him are the salt of the earth.

It was a sad day when I left Carrow Road, and so unfortunate that in the season Norwich won the Milk Cup the bitter pill of relegation had to be swallowed as well. And it was bitter. Norwich went down through absolutely ludicrous circumstances. If the Football League ever allow such a situation to happen again then we might as well pack the game in. It's not sour grapes from me. I've moved on, and from my career point of view it doesn't really matter. But for Coventry to play their last game weeks after everyone else has finished, allowing them to escape the drop, and for Luton to face them after an end-of-season break in Spain, was a disgrace.

I'm not saying Luton didn't try, but it was a vital League game for Coventry and it's not quite the same as playing it during the season. Then to cap it all Everton put virtually a reserve side out for Coventry's very last game and lost 4–0. The League champions had only gone down by that score once all season, on the opening day against Tottenham. And Coventry had forgotten what it was like to win three games on the trot before that last escape route was mapped out so conveniently for them. It just shouldn't have been on.

You're messing with people's careers, condemning Norwich to go down instead of Coventry just because of a phoney, after-season bunch of games that only one club wanted to win. Good players like Dave Watson and Chris Woods had their England chances put at risk by having to play in the Second Division. The Canaries shouldn't have gone down. The club could have lost those players, and indeed had a struggle to convince Woods and Steve Bruce that they should stay, when bigger First Division clubs were ready to offer them a more glamorous future.

If the League ever allow those conditions to prevail again, they are making a complete mockery of the promotion and relegation system. The League championship becomes a total farce. Whatever anyone says, Norwich City went down and they should *not* have been relegated. It wasn't even that the club played badly and deserved to go down. We had an awful lot of injury problems. Then missing out on Europe (through the UEFA ban on English clubs), after having qualified by winning the Milk Cup, was the last straw.

I was none too happy, either, with a further example of Ken Brown's irresolution. The season had been finished well over a month and we were in the middle of June – just two days before I was due for one of my close-season trips to New Zealand – when the Norwich manager told me I was getting a free transfer. I was contractually committed to New Zealand, but had no time to sort myself out with another club. So I had no job to come back to and was out of the country thousands of miles away when I needed to be showing my face back home and reminding people I could stilll play.

In life, however, we all have a few moans and groans, and I must say that Ken Brown is a smashing fellow both as a person and a manager. He picked me for the team; gave me the freedom to play the game as I wanted; and let me enjoy myself on the park. I loved it at Norwich. I had two and a half refreshing years at the club.

Ken's West Ham upbringing really pays off because he encourages everyone to play in an entertaining way. That's why Norwich have such a loyal following of hardcore supporters who know they'll get value for money from the team.

I hope I repaid the supporters' faith, and like to think I had something to do with Norwich signing the player whose contribution to the club winning the Milk Cup was so great. I had been at Carrow Road a year, and it was at the club's Christmas dinner for the players that I had an idea about who might ideally suit us. We had been going well – lying in the top eight of the First Division – but we were flat to the boards in terms of strength in depth. All the lads were working and training hard but we had problems. Mark Barham, who I think is top class, had got a very bad knee injury and was side-lined for a long time. There was Dave Watson, whom I regard as the best defender in the country, and goalkeeper Chris Woods, who is potentially the best in his position, playing out of their skins and being a great example to everyone.

I went to Ken Brown and told him we needed an injection of new blood. I said: 'If you go and buy Asa Hartford or Tony Grealish (who was at Brighton at the time) it will just give us that little bit of steel and a new face that could take us into Europe for the first time.' (Ken couldn't do anything at that time, but peculiarly the following year he ended up signing Asa and the rest is history.)

Apart from the likes of Woods and Watson, whom you can build a team around, there were plenty of characters at Norwich during my stay. One of the most pleasant guys you could ever wish to meet is striker John Deehan. He's probably found the perfect niche for himself at Norwich, the club I fondly call the Village Green team of football because of its homely touch (a contrast to the high-powered finance of Manchester City and Lawrie McMenemy's superstar syndrome at Southampton).

I can see why John struggled at West Brom and Aston Villa. It was probably all right for him when he was a kid because there was no real pressure. But when you're expected to come up with the goods week in and week out, it's very hard at those types of clubs – I know because I experienced it at Manchester City. John found he was wanted at Norwich and felt part of the team. He had a good sense of humour as well. When the main stand burned down at Carrow Road the gossip in the training-ground dressing room next morning was all centred on what had happened. The next minute, Dixie Deehan had run in with a fireman's uniform on . . . and a watering can! The lads were creased up. It was the sort of situation when you've got to try and make light of a disaster. John has his own radio programme in Norwich with a sports slot and he plays a few records.

Dixie's fellow striker, Keith Bertschin, was another smashing lad who was there for eighteen months of my stay. We had some blinding times on trips, especially when we kept going to . . . Norway. No, it's not exactly the mecca of football, but we had the Norwegian international defender Aage Hareide with the club at the time, so we were always an attraction in his country. We'd be off there at every opportunity. Aage was pretty ordinary as a player but he had a great heart and was a good competitor. I used to say to him: 'I bet you get down on your hands and knees every day and say "Thank God I'm Norwegian", because you would never, ever have played for a proper football country!'

Put different characters like these together and you have a good team. I like to think I could play a bit myself, then Asa Hartford came – and suddenly the team that went on to win the Milk Cup was being blended.

What can I say about Asa? As I've already described, we had our moments together at Manchester City. He was a fine Scottish international, and, as befits his race, has probably still got his first wage packet – his pockets always seemed to be sewn up on pay day!

Asa lived in Wilmslow, Cheshire, and I was based in Southampton so we used to converge on Norwich on a Wednesday from different directions to prepare for Saturday games.

I couldn't have lived in Norwich, even though the people were friendly, because I was only on a monthly contract. Of course, my interest in horse-racing was well served with Newmarket being just down the road from Norwich. But I had my stud farm at Southampton that needed constant attention. My business life still flowed from Southampton. I could have been out on my ear at any moment, so it made no sense to make a permanent move to Norfolk.

The travelling did take its toll – the Mercedes blew up with 186,000 miles on the clock – though I'll admit I don't treat cars with the same loving attention I give to my horses. (Even after I left Norwich and went fairly close to home with the move to Portsmouth, I would reckon to do around 35,000 miles a year in the car with my racing interests. I really am the Man on the Run!)

When I had to stay overnight in Norwich, it was at the charming, little Oaklands Hotel and, typically of Norwich, I was always made very welcome. The owner George Dack loved his horses and I kept tipping him losers. I don't know why he kept putting me up! I enjoyed being there – and if you are always fair with people and you feel wanted, you'll do a good job.

I never did a better job than going to Wembley with Norwich – and sneaking my eleven-year-old son Michael into the great stadium and on to the Norwich bench for the Milk Cup final. Just getting there – beating our East Anglian rivals Ipswich Town 2–0 in the second leg of the semi-final – was an unforgettable occasion. Dixie Deehan and Steve Bruce got the goals then, and we were carried off shoulder-high. That didn't even happen when I was with Southampton and we beat Manchester United for the FA Cup. The whole city of Norwich went wild. Everyone wanted tickets for the Wembley final against Sunderland. We were in demand for personal appearances, and fixed up with new suits for the big day: all the trappings of a club that had got to a big final.

It was then I got the thought: a great day, a Sunday afternoon kick-off, why don't I get my lad Michael in and on the bench? So I got a professional golfer friend of mine,

David Allen, to station Michael outside the players' entrance as the Norwich team coach drew up at Wembley. There was a huge crowd milling around outside, so as I got off the coach, I grabbed Michael and David and rushed them both inside – no questions asked, even by the security people who make Wembley a fortress on big occasions like these.

I had mentioned to Ken Brown that I would like my lad on the bench if at all possible and, bless him, he said it was fine. I'm sure that no other manager would have allowed it – and I will always love Ken Brown for that. The club does belong to the people and I hope they never lose the warmth they showed me that day.

Michael was wearing his Norwich tracksuit. He couldn't believe that he was actually out there and part of the great occasion. To this day he says to me: 'I can't remember anything about it, Dad.' It passed him by, which it does for a player as well. My thirteen-year-old daughter, Nicola, wasn't to be outdone either. She had yellow-and-green colouring sprayed on her hair. To anyone else she would have looked like some outrageous punk, but to her family she was gorgeous.

Young Michael watched us beat Sunderland 1–0 from the bench in front of the Royal Box, and then did the lap of honour with me. I can't think a father and son have ever had more fun together at Wembley. I was lucky that no one else in the team had a grown-up son, so I wasn't stepping on anyone else's toes or denying anyone else a privilege. Of course, if there had been a few of us in the same position with big lads as sons, it would have been out of the question. But then again, I've been pretty fortunate throughout my life. Michael was ten at the time, old enough to know how to behave himself. A couple of the reserve lads knew him and looked after him – it was marvellous.

The triumphant team went back to Norwich for a civic reception the next day, and even though the weather was terrible and the rain hammered down there was a tremendous turn-out to welcome us home. I didn't know then that I'd played my last game for Norwich City, but I couldn't think of a more enjoyable way to say goodbye to the Village Green people.

15 · Hooked on Horses

I blame Lester Piggott for getting me hooked on horse-racing. However, when one of his unique finishes landed me my first betting coup as a pimply youth, I could never have dreamed I would get so involved in the sport of kings as I have done . . . going on to become an owner and breeder.

These days I'm probably as well known for my involvement with horses as I am for any deeds on the football pitch. But I've always had the good luck to have been able to combine the two without harming either. I like to think that my professional attitude to football spills over into my racing involvement. Fortunes can be won by breeding the next Derby winner, but that's as likely as being struck twice in your life by lightning or winning the pools two weeks running. Many owners with huge stakes in racing have tried all their lives for the classic winner and never come up with it. In this game it is all too easy to get your fingers burned, and the headaches are plentiful.

Despite all the drawbacks, horses are the love of my life, and I couldn't imagine life without looking forward to a day at the races. I suppose that racing started to seep into my blood as a boy because there was a horse-racing yard just over the hill from my home village of Orcheston. It was run by a well-known old figure in the game, trainer Richmond Sturdy.

In that kind of environment everyone seems to have a tip for a horse or purports to know what is going on behind the scenes. But as I found out to my cost later on in life, there is no such thing as a sure tip – and not too many people know what is going on! At that stage I don't know whether my interest was in horses, or the girls who looked after them. At fourteen or fifteen boys tend to hang around the local places of interest and in this case it was a racing stable.

Then, not long after I signed for Southampton, came my first real venture into the world of betting on horses. A girl from the Sturdy yard gave me a tip for a horse, Tintagel II, in a big race, the Ebor Handicap. She also said that Lester Piggott would ride it – before he was even booked. So I shot up to the bookies and had what for me at the time was a big bet – £8 to win £100. Sure enough, a week later Lester was booked to ride the horse, the odds came tumbling down to 6–1 and it bolted in. I don't know whether that was a good thing, because it might have cured me if I'd lost. Suddenly the race game seemed easy, if only for a day!

I can be interested and participate in racing until the day I die, while football is bound to give me up before very much longer as a player. I can look after horses and perhaps keep a couple of brood mares until they put me in a box, although I know it's not the cheapest of hobbies. It's the challenge that I love. In football I always wanted to be the best: in racing I want to breed the best – something that's better than great owner–breeders like Lord Derby, The Queen or Robert Sangster can produce.

I started to think how great it would be to own a horse and at the first opportunity, with a few extra quid in my pocket, I took the plunge. At the age of twenty-four, the only possessions I had in my life were an Austin A35 car . . . and half a horse. I was spending all my spare money on the upkeep of both, and the four-legged animal was more expensive.

I bought my first horse off a character called Ken Payne, who was renowned for his betting coups when he trained a lot of winners up in the north. He had started out with a yard in West Wellow, near Southampton, and a good jockey friend of mine, Frank Morby, said that Ken had some fair yearlings. I respected Frank's judgement. We used to go racing a lot before he went off to Kenya and became champion jockey and trainer over there. Frank said that maybe it was worth going to have a look at them.

Ken had three yearlings for me to see, and I had a rough idea about what the price would be because I knew how much he had paid for them in the Newcastle sales, 380 guineas apiece. The one I bought was a little filly called Cathy Jane – and I could never have known what a treasure she would turn out to be. Everything I have achieved in racing is down to her – even though her downright bad temper once gave me one of the most painful injuries I've suffered in my career! But more of that later.

My Southampton team mate at that time, Brian O'Neil, was a partner in the ownership and we sent her to Bill Wightman, a trainer from whom I learned so much about racehorses and their training. Bill is one of the old school. Along with Neville Crump, he is the most senior man around in his profession. Bill trained at Upham, near Southampton. His skill as a trainer is probably the reason why I'm still so involved in racing today, because the mare Cathy Jane turned out to be good enough to win four races. She won three handicaps as a four-year-old, including the Brown Jack Stakes at Ascot on King George VI and Queen Elizabeth II Diamond Stakes day.

Brian O'Neil and I hardly had two bob to rub together after we'd paid the expenses for owning the horse, but my gambling instincts told me to go for a horse rather than the security of bricks and mortar. It's not so safe, but a whole lot more fun.

I could never forget that 1973 summer's day when Cathy Jane won the Brown Jack, one of the longest staying races on the calendar. It was during pre-season training at Southampton and we had been sent on a cross-country run of about ten miles in the morning. I had tailed off at the back and I'm sure that Brian wasn't very far ahead. It was a struggle for me that day, probably after too good a time the night before! It certainly left us short of time to get to Ascot and we fairly raced from Southampton's training ground to get to the races for the off. Consequently we weren't as smartly dressed as we wanted to be. I had an open-neck shirt with jacket and casual trousers. Bill Wightman, on the other hand, was looking really dapper as befits a successful trainer. He was wearing a smart trilby hat and looked every inch the top trainer of handicappers.

Brian O'Neil and I looked a little bit dishevelled, to say the least, when we arrived at the track for the parade ring before the big race. Willie Carson was riding for us. (It was a great season for him, which eventually led to his first success as champion jockey.) Willie was ready to do the business and there were Brian and I looking as though we'd been blown in by the wind, rather than the owners. Anyway, Willie had already been given his instructions and I just added: 'All the best.' My partner then issued the greatest riding orders I've ever heard given to a future champion jockey. Brian said to Willie: 'Don't forget, Willie, you're a cowboy – and the rest are Indians!'

Willie's always been a chirpy sort and he replied: 'You two lads look a bit rough.' I retorted: 'If you'd worked as hard as we have this morning, Willie, you would look rough as well.'

The race went perfectly and Cathy Jane won by a head from a very good staying horse, Cumbernauld, ridden by Tony Murray. But from Swinley Bottom, about a mile from the finish, Willie was riding Cathy Jane for all he was worth, pushing and scrubbing along.

Brian and I got down to the winners' enclosure to welcome Cathy Jane back. It was a super performance, because she'd been under pressure from such a long way out. Willie came back in, rolled off the horse and exclaimed: 'Don't ever tell me about your being knackered – this is the hardest ride I've ever had in my life!' He could hardly catch his breath, and I don't think any other jockey could have won on her that day. He just wouldn't give in and neither would she, as she just kept finding that extra little bit to win. That was probably her best and hardest run, and I never thought she'd race again. I've still got pictures of her with weals on her backside that you wouldn't believe, stick marks from where Willie had had to keep her going.

The satisfaction of winning a good race at Ascot was tremendous. The prize money was about £1,600, pretty sizeable all those years ago, when the training fees were probably £20 a week compared to £130 these days. And to show how tough she was, Cathy Jane went out and won again. It was another good, staying handicap race, the Stonehill Handicap at Goodwood.

As a two-year-old Cathy Jane had been very backward and we didn't really bother with her, apart from one run at the back end of the season over six furlongs. My mate Frank Morby rode her and told me that he didn't think she was much good. For once I didn't take his advice – simply because I couldn't get rid of her. Most of the sales were over so I was really stuck with her for another year. I committed the cardinal sin of saying we would give her time until she was a three-year-old, only four months away, and then expected results straight away. I was ready to sell her and we didn't really know what was her best distance.

Cathy Jane went in a selling plate race at Newmarket that I thought she could win, and she finished second. My immediate thought was to get rid of her. Bill Wightman said that was OK, and put her in for the Ascot Sales, but asked me whether I would mind if he entered her for the odd race. I said that was fair enough, because he had a month before the sales. Bill switched her from a mile and a quarter to two miles and she ran an absolute blinder in a decent race at Wolverhampton, finishing fourth. Then she ran at Bath with that fine jockey Joe Mercer booked to ride, at the course where he was so good it was always reckoned he had a head start on anyone.

Brian O'Neil and I went down to Bath, along with our Southampton team mate Jim Steele, who was really just along for a good day out. I stuck £3 on Cathy to win at 7–1.

I hadn't got much more on me. Brian didn't have a bet and Jim backed a horse in the same race called Eleanor Queen. As they came to the finish, out of a dog leg three-quarters of a furlong out, Eleanor Queen was on the rails coming up to challenge us. The favourite, Oyster Bar, was on the outside. All of a sudden Oyster Bar veered right across the course, bumped into our horse and that took us into Eleanor Queen, just after we'd got the better of her.

I had been roaring home Cathy Jane in the stands and we crossed the line second. I hoped that an objection would give us the race. As we got to the unsaddling enclosure Joe Mercer arrived to tell us: 'Don't worry boys, you'll get this,' upon which we didn't see Jim Steele for dust. He'd shot round to the bookies to try and bet on the objection that we'd get the race. I wasn't too bothered about that – all I wanted was for my horse to get the verdict. It all worked out well and we were awarded the race. Then we knew that Cathy Jane needed a long trip and she went on from there as a four-year-old winning those three races for us.

On another occasion I remember we weren't that well dressed for glorious Goodwood. I turned up wearing jeans and a T-shirt, not quite the gear for the owners' enclosure at that particular racecourse. Lawrie McMenemy had not long joined Southampton and was making us train in the afternoon. I had said to Lawrie that I had a horse running and I was going racing. Brian O'Neil couldn't go, but probably because I was the blue-eyed boy I was excused training. Our jockey that day was little Chris Leonard, an apprentice whose stick was almost bigger than he was. I'll never forget Bill Wightman's instructions as the little fellow stood there trembling. We were up against a horse called Eric who had easily won his previous race. Bill said: 'Now, young man, whatever Eric does I want you to sit two lengths behind him and then two furlongs from home pull your filly out and give her a smack – but only give her one.' Chris rode a perfect race and sure enough pulled her out at the right time. I watched through the field-glasses as Chris gave the filly a tap. I put down the glasses and said: 'I won't need these any more!' Sure enough she stormed home, winning by a length and a half, with me giving her a right shout to the line.

Since Goodwood, Cathy Jane has been the backbone of my breeding operation. She's quite well bred on her dam's side and was by an Italian Derby-winner Lauso.

I thought at the time of Cathy Jane's successes as a four-year-old that I might not be able to afford another horse so I might as well breed with her. I sent Cathy Jane to a decent, little seven-furlong handicap horse, Mandamus, and she bred a colt called Man on the Run. He wasn't a particularly good-looking colt, but he was a tough little bugger – just like his mum. Man on the Run eventually won six races: three on the Flat and three jumping, and was placed twenty-odd times. He was very one paced, like I am today, but he could battle on and we had some marvellous fun with him.

Man on the Run was trained by Bill Wightman. He was placed as a two-year-old and won at three. He was still in training as a four-year-old and we went back to Bath, where he was ridden by that brilliant young jockey Billy Newnes. Billy was an apprentice at the time and set off in front of a pretty large field with another horse, Systems Analysis, close up. These two went eight lengths clear going down the back of the track, and I remember starting to shout mine home from the bottom turn at Bath, four furlongs from home. Brian O'Neil – who was still involved in the ownership – Alan Ball and I roared him home.

It was nip and tuck all the way to the line, and Billy Newnes rode a blinder to win by a head. The first two were twelve lengths clear of the rest. I went to the winners' enclosure a very excited man. I'm probably one of the most enthusiastic owners you'll see, and I'll shout my horse home with the best of them. In fact, I'll apologize now for my language to anyone who has been within earshot of me when a horse of mine has a winning chance. I ran round to welcome my horse, and Bill Wightman, as smartly dressed as ever, said quite calmly: 'Michael, I've discovered something about your horse today. He loves to be shouted at!' We broke out laughing.

Both Kevin Keegan and Brian O'Neil had shares in Man on the Run, so named after a BBC South television documentary about me at the time Cathy Jane foaled her colt. We thought it would be a good name for the horse, and eventually this book! Like Cathy Jane, he owes me absolutely nothing, the £500 stud fee being repaid many times over.

Cathy Jane was then covered by a horse called Hot Spark to produce the colt Hot Trail, and I sold him as a yearling for £4,600. Hot Trail ended up winning three races as a two-year-old and three handicaps on the trot as a three-year-old. He won about £10,000 in prize money, but then had an unfortunate accident when he broke down as a three-year-old running for the first time over hurdles, on hard ground. I always maintain the connections were mad to have risked him in such conditions, because he was a topping little horse who would have always won races.

Cathy Jane's next offspring was by a sprinter called Song, for a £1,000 stud fee, and this one was the biggest horse I'd seen. I sold him to one of my best friends, Phil Trant, a road engineering contractor who was to die in a car accident. He called the horse Kerry Tune, because he was from that part of Ireland, but as it turned out this colt was the only one of Cathy Jane's produce that appeared on the racetrack not to win. In fact, he ended up being unsound and had to be put down.

Cathy Jane's next produce was by Bill Wightman's very good sprint-handicapper, Import. If Cathy Jane has had a fault it's that she's been very irregular as a breeder, producing every other year. I'd had no luck with her for a couple of years, so I sent her up to a good friend of mine in Yorkshire, Bob Urquhart, to be looked after. That was where she foaled my best horse yet, Jamesmead.

Jamesmead is not top class, but he is a good handicapper.

All Cathy Jane's horses have a tough streak in them, even though commercially she's not worth two bob. She's just not fashionably bred. But Jamesmead has won over £34,000, which is not bad for a £500 stud fee. He finished second in the Cesarewitch, which is one of the leading flat-race handicaps near the end of the season. (Indeed, had there not been a withdrawal of a horse on the morning of the race, which messed up the weights and caused a furore at the time, Jamesmead might well have won.) He's also run in a lot of good hurdle races and is a very decent horse. Cathy Jane's always had a bit of temperament about her, but that's probably what has made her so good. When she's got a foal around her she can be particularly bad tempered and once when I was showing some people round I got too close and she took a lump out of my shoulder! It was my fault, I got a bit cocky, but when she turned on me I thought my arm was broken at first. She pulled off a piece of skin the size of a 50 pence coin from my arm – it was like a nasty grass burn. But her nose punched me at the same time, so it was like getting a dead leg and having skin ripped off at the same time. She's never been any different, a tough old sort who has never wanted any friends. She doesn't want you to be nice to her – just feed her and leave her alone. But unless fillies are tough with a bit of spirit about them, they aren't much good. And to be fair to her, I've been around many times when she hasn't gone for me.

Now we're hoping for more success with her next produce, by a nice horse called Swing Easy. She's only ever had colts and I'd like to think she might have a filly this time – I'd like to keep one if she does, and race her. Then perhaps she could take up where Cathy Jane leaves off.

In the early days I used to get involved with a few syndicates, where a bunch of people club together to buy a horse. One of these syndicates was with some fellow footballers like Peter Shilton and Alan Ball, and we bought a little filly called Spill the Beans. The syndicate was run by a former England

Youth goalie, Bob Charles, and a taxi driver well known in Southampton as Larry the Cab. Spill the Beans was a good name for a horse because these two were the biggest gossips in Southampton. They would know everything that was going on. Unfortunately that filly broke her knee and had to be put down. But she ran twice and was placed both times.

In another syndicate we paid £6,000 for a horse called Spark Off, each member putting in around £750. It was trained down in Devon by my good friend John Baker. Spark Off had won on the Flat before we bought him. He was a good little horse and he was schooled over fences. We ran him at Chepstow in a televised race and naturally the syndicate lads were very excited. They all had their £5, £10 and £20 each-way bets, some of them a good bit more, and we had a top jockey in Jonjo O'Neill to ride. The horse just did not jump a hurdle, and nearly pulled up at one. I've never been so embarrassed in all my life. I couldn't make it out. He had run too badly to be true and was completely tailed off.

Back at John Baker's yard they couldn't understand it, because the horse had worked so well at home. I said that next time Spark Off ran we should make sure of his jumping. We took him to Taunton racetrack and schooled him round the fences there with another horse and he worked really well. In fact, he worked so nicely I thought he only had to jump round next time and he was a cert. But I decided to keep that to myself. I couldn't tell the others because no one would have believed me. If I'd told the syndicate members he was a good thing I would have been frightened to death that the same thing would happen as in his first flop for us. All I had was my own private confidence that comes from seeing something with one's own eyes.

Southampton were playing Arsenal on New Year's Day morning, kick-off eleven o'clock. Lawrie McMenemy had taken us away to the Southampton Post House overnight. I had asked Bob Charles to put my money on for me, in bits and pieces all over town. That was because I wanted the best possible price and didn't want the news of one big bet to get back to the racetrack bookies, who would have immediately cut back the odds. At little tracks like Devon and Exeter, a £200 bet on a horse can make it go from 20–1 to 3–1 favourite. I raised every penny I could lay my hands on to back the horse, including loans from my father and brother.

I asked Bob to come to our hotel at eight o'clock for the money. In betting circles today it was not a great deal, but then it was still a hefty piece of change to me. If he had gone straight round to one of the big bookmakers' chains with £600 to slap down they would not have wanted to accept the bet. I know that from experience! I'm not a great expert in betting like Bob who had put tenners and twenties all over Southampton on Spark Off.

Strangely enough, every meeting in the country was off that day except Devon and Exeter. The Saints had played our game against Arsenal on a rock-hard pitch at The Dell and I couldn't believe the meeting was still on. Apparently the West Country was just mild enough for the races to go ahead. We had lost the game 1–0, and I stood in the players' room at Southampton, beckoning Larry the Cab and Alan Ball. I said: 'I want you to come with me now, I've got a horse for you to back.' We went into a betting shop and they both had around £20 on Spark Off. It stormed in at 12–1.

I often wonder about keeping quiet with most of the syndicate lads, who would have wanted to tear me limb from limb if they had thought I had held information back from them on having a big bet. But I just didn't want to get egg all over my face again. Spark Off did win a few races afterwards, but didn't come up to expectations.

On that day I won more than seven thousand pounds, probably the most I've ever won on a bet. These days I'll have a hundred or a couple of hundred on my own horses if I feel they have a chance, but I very rarely bet on other people's, apart from just having a simple interest in a race.

Not everything in racing is rosy – far from it. In fact, as a man who has travelled all over the world and visited racecourses wherever I've stopped off, I can say we've got just about the worst facilities I've come across. It often surprises me that the punters in this country put up with such poor treatment. We've got the best racing, and possibly the best horses in the world, but for the punter who helps pay the betting tax and horse-racing levy, conditions are atrocious. Our attitude seems to be that because we are British we do everything right – I think that's totally wrong. Australia, New Zealand, South Africa and the United States are all far superior horse-racing countries in terms of spectator comforts. In the not-too-distant future, the racing authorities have got to look after the man in the street a lot more.

I'm a great believer in all-weather tracks. Why should racing be off just because of a bit of frost? Floodlit tracks should be introduced for more night racing. For the industry to grow and prosper I believe there is a market for such developments. I'm not saying we should mess about with the Derby and the other great classic races. They will always be there. But if there is a market for something else, for a different kind of racing, it has got to be looked into. Don't say it all costs too much when there are millions going to the Government in betting taxes.

Looking long term, if some of the revenues generated by the sport were ploughed back into providing better facilities, there would be more racing, it would be more popular and the Governement could still rake in the levels of taxation that they get now. I know that racing is basically a rich man's game, but the betting levy is an important source of income for the Exchequer so the ordinary people are important. We won't get people going to races if the facilities are bad. We are light years behind other countries, and that's what worries me. At nearly every one of our tracks the catering facilities, the bars and the viewing of races are all extremely poor. Food and drink, even if rarely up to standard, are scandalously priced compared with the outside world. They don't try and rip off the punters abroad. Why do we have to be the only big racing country who do not give a fair deal to spectators?

Here endeth my sermon on racing – but I will still go and I will continue to breed horses because I love them. Just the thought of breeding something that could beat one of Robert Sangster's million-pound animals gives me a special thrill. I just love the competition that I've carried over from the football world to racing. What the future holds I don't know, but I'm sure I'll be around horses for a long time to come. It's my only other main interest apart from football.

16 · The Art of Scoring

I'm proud of the fact that I have scored more goals in my career than anyone else currently playing in the Football League. I passed the milestone of 300 senior goals back in November 1984, appropriately for Norwich in the Milk Cup, which we won. Of course, the luck I've had in being able to play longer than most people around has been a major contributory factor towards this record. However, I like to think that I know what it takes to make a consistent goalscorer.

I've had the good fortune throughout my career to play with and against many great scorers, and I hope learned something from all of them. For instance, I've been in the playing company of stars such as Geoff Hurst, Allan Clarke, Martin Chivers, Ron Davies, Ted MacDougall, Malcolm Macdonald and Jimmy Greaves – all naturals when it came to sticking the ball away. These great goalscorers all had one thing in common . . . a gambler's instinct. They are the ones who think the ball is going to go under someone's foot, bounce over a player's head, or they think someone's going to miss it – and so let them in.

There are two different types of striker: the out-and-out goalscorers, and the match winners. There are goalscorers who will notch a couple when their team gets beaten 4–2, or they'll grab a hat-trick in a 5–0 win – all very nice. Then there are the all-important match winners who score when you win 1–0, or pop up with a point-saver in a 1–1 draw. This type of scorer is priceless. If you can combine him with the one who sprays goals all over the place, win, lose or draw, you have a formidable creature.

I believe I was at my peak in the years 1974 to 1976. I was an England regular, and the national side should have gone to the World Cup finals in 1974. I spent most of that time in the Second Division with Southampton, so I found it a doddle to knock in twenty goals a season. They were the easy years. I had the pace to go by people, skill on the ball and I was blessed with the knack of scoring. But most importantly, I had a sense of humour to go with those attributes, an ability to laugh at myself. To score a lot of goals a player must never be afraid to try the impossible, and that brings out the natural gambling instincts in the breed.

I've played with far better goalscorers than myself, but I was born with a natural fitness. Coach Lew Chatterley used to say to me at Southampton: 'How good a player could you have been if you had trained?' My answer to that was: 'I'd have probably been finished at twenty-eight.' I've always been very lazy and never practised my shooting. A lot of my football has been purely spontaneous, off-the-cuff stuff. I don't plan it or try to understand it.

I've played with lots of goalscorers in my time but not many match winners. I was a match winner, especially at Southampton in my formative years. I used to score when we won 1–0, more often than not when we played away with that famous 1–9–1 system that failed to catch on. I was the one all on my own up front.

Ron Davies was a great goalscorer from my earlier days, but probably the best at simply sticking the ball in the net was Ted MacDougall, who was with me during my second spell with the Saints. He would score hat-tricks in 5–0 wins, but a match winner is somebody who doesn't touch the ball for 89 minutes then suddenly beats two opponents and scores. Ted could only fire the gun, a match winner is somebody who can load and fire. George Best was one, and Chelsea's David Speedie is showing he can fulfil that requirement these days.

Jimmy, Greaves, my television colleague these days, was a goalscorer rather than a match winner. Of course, his goals still won plenty of matches, but he wasn't always the kind who would snap up the crucial strikes. Malcolm Macdonald would also come into that category, in my opinion. My idea of a perfect match winner was Allan Clarke when Leeds United were at their best. His type would nearly always score in a 1–0 win or be around to snatch a late equalizer.

The most potent attacking force occurs when the natural goalscorer and the match winner come in pairs. The goalscorer tends to complement his team mates more than the match winner, who can be a bit of a loner. The goalscorer can often be a robust sort – although Greaves was a notable exception – a big striker who can hold a team together and puts himself about. He knocks balls off and gets in important flicks in the danger area. But the match winner is probably an individualist, who flits in, reads a situation in a flash and suddenly the ball is in the net.

Ian Rush is probably the most prolific goalscorer around today, who can also win games, and it certainly helps that he has been playing for what I consider to be the best team around, Liverpool. Gary Lineker at Everton is certainly developing into that combination of natural scorer and regular match winner. A lot of that improvement is because he left Leicester and went to a team that gave him far more control and much better support. He's always in there nicking half-chances and picking up the pieces. At Filbert Street he was more of a straightforward taker of clear chances. Put him through on goal and he would score nearly every time. Now he's added an ability to be more crafty and cunning, and he's a more complete player.

Mark Hughes is still very much a beginner, although he's had a meteoric rise at Manchester United, causing Barcelona to go in for him. Potentially, Mark can become a world-class striker, but I'd like to see him do it for a couple of years before I make a final judgement on him.

I am often asked if I envy the current crop of British

strikers, who seem to be top of the popularity stakes with the big, rich clubs in Italy and Spain. Playing on the Continent is a chance for people like Mark Hateley, Ray Wilkins, Liam Brady, Trevor Francis and Steve Archibald to insure their futures with fabulous wages. In my time I did have the opportunity to go abroad, to play in France, but I decided to go to Manchester City instead. Perhaps if I had been born ten or twelve years later the pressure on me to go abroad would have been more intense, especially as these days British clubs can't afford to turn down transfer fees running into millions from the Italians and Spanish clubs.

However, I don't regret staying in England. I've always earned good money from the game in this country. Football has come easy to me, and that's not meant to sound arrogant or cocky. Earning money has never been a problem, and I'm in the incredibly lucky position of never having been really short of the stuff. If I wanted a suit and it cost £300 I've had it, there has never been the need to check to see if I can afford something. All right, perhaps I haven't been in a position to go out and lay down £50,000 on a Rolls-Royce – I've had to make do with a Mercedes – but I've always been prepared to roll up my sleeves and work at any project I go in for.

I never particularly wanted to go abroad to play just for the money. I've always wanted to earn money, and there's no crime in that, but I've wanted to do it and play football in the environment that suits *me*. My life isn't just about football. It's about my horses and everything concerning their upkeep and well being. And even in football I've never fancied being told by the likes of Brian Clough where I've got to play, or have Terry Venables saying I must do something a certain way. I've always played the game my way.

I've been able to retain a little bit of my own identity within the game, regardless of what a manager says. I know you've got to fit within a general team pattern, but apart from that I've done what I wanted to do. That's been my kick out of life. It's why I've been able to keep playing for so long, because my interest hasn't wavered too much. I know that the argument for playing abroad is: go for the money and you'll never have to worry again. But I wouldn't want to do anything, even for two or three years, where I wasn't in total control of my own destiny and actually liking what I was doing. I'd never be able to replace those few years spent away from my natural habitat. You don't get a second chance in life, I'd never get those few years back.

Sometimes you have to do little things you don't particularly want to do, perhaps going abroad to earn money for a matter of one or two weeks. But to go to Saudi Arabia or other desert countries, like quite a few of our managers have done in recent years, is not for me. Malcolm Allison, Keith Burkinshaw and the rest can keep their well-paid jobs in the Middle East, I don't think it's worth a chunk out of my life. I don't want to opt out in the way Don Revie or Dave Mackay have. I know they've got families to keep and responsibilities, but to say they can go off for three or four years and come back and be happy – that's rubbish.

The thought of going to Italy and being locked away in a training camp for days on end fills me with loathing. If I'm playing on a Saturday I nearly always have an early night on Friday and I wouldn't do much on a Thursday either. I don't need to be made to live like a monk to be a decent player. I've always been able to enjoy myself earlier in the week and have never been stopped going racing on a Thursday or Friday if I wanted to. I would never have wanted to change that and I could never have played in a system where the players have to be packed off to some kind of prison, like naughty kids, to make sure they don't get out of condition. I've always taken a certain amount of pride in my fitness, any self-respecting professional sportsman should do that or get out. Being a good pro is being able to live with yourself and know that on a Saturday afternoon, from three o'clock to twenty to five, you can go out there and give your 100 per cent.

17 · The Conscience of the Game

It's not the state of football that bothers me so much as the conscience of the sport I love. The game is just the same as it has ever been, but the people have changed. We are getting more and more coaches who have swallowed the rule book and they have given the game indigestion. They are playing the percentage game – get the ball in the opposing penalty box fifty times and you'll have so many occasions when your side will win the ball in there. Then a certain percentage of those occasions will end up with a shot at goal, and a certain number of those will be successful.

All this means that more and more teams are playing to win free-kicks and long throw-ins. Football has become a game of pressure in those conditions, and certain clubs have to be criticized for encouraging this cold, statistical way of approaching matches.

These clubs are actually competing . . . by *not* competing! They've looked at the game and said: 'We can't go out and buy the likes of Bryan Robson, Chris Waddle and Peter Shilton. We can't compete in the transfer market for that sort of player. But what we can do is field a team of fit, strong lads with average ability who can be reasonably well organized to defend. Then we get the ball in the opposing half as quickly as we possibly can, push up and squeeze the game into a very small area and rely on set pieces – corners, free-kicks, and long throw-ins. Put in someone who is big and good in the air and we won't need a lot of players with the skill to go by people.

Sheffield Wednesday, Watford and Wimbledon have been the brand leaders of this kind of football. However, it's hard to argue that they'll be the death of the game, because that style has brought their success. Wimbledon are a great example of this syndrome and the club that I've had the most recent experience of, having played against them in the Second Division promotion battle in 1985–6. They were just non-Leaguers a while back. Although I have every respect for the way they have advanced themselves all the way to the First Division, I think that basically they are a team of bullies. Of course, they have adapted to a situation where they have to exist on pitifully poor gates, paying modest wages to players. You don't get the best players without paying the best rates.

I am still optimistic enough to think that football will overcome this steadily increasing style of aerial combat, where the ball has to plead for mercy because it is getting such a hammering. There are still enough sides and sufficient players who want to play attractive football the way it was meant to be played: teams who want to encourage wingers to get down the byline and ask their players to show the skills of beating a man. They want to show attractive build-ups to moves and have shots from the edge of penalty-box. You can get plenty of goal-mouth excitement without having to hoick the ball fifty or sixty yards in the general direction of the penalty area.

There's a little bit more to the game than simply putting the opposition under pressure by relying on strength of numbers. Don't get me wrong, I'm not saying it doesn't work – because it surely does. But it's a style that suits the bullies of the game. The teams which play it invariably have big, strong players who want to impose their physical will on others. They do intimidate other teams, and it is a very hard system to play against. That's what I call competing by

What soccer can do without

not competing. They can get any Joe Soap in football to play their way.

I remain convinced that we have world-class players in British domestic football. And I think that our club football is without any question the best in the world. Everyone knocks us to be sure – but try to get a Brazilian master to cope with the change in conditions that we have to face week in and week out. Just this last season I've gone from playing on a pitch that was flooded and ankle deep in mud – how they got the game on I don't know – to the following midweek on a bone-hard surface when the game should have been called off because of the heavy frost. I don't think Pele or Platini have had to put up with those sort of restrictions.

English football will survive. We are as good as anyone in the world. We can beat the best in the world both at international and especially club level. Our football is healthy in that sense, and will remain so provided that there are still teams who are prepared to let the skilful players express themselves and put up with a few of the eccentrics who probably over-elaborate and overdo the entertainment side of things. Used in the right way such players can be a great asset to a team. We must tolerate the few luxury players and encourage managers to keep faith with them. What we mustn't do is to keep knocking our star players. If you've got a star – let him get on with it and run the show. That's what the people want to see, not some zombie playing to a restricted system.

I'm totally against what I call the Communist approach to football. I'm talking about the people who want all their players to be equal; to be all paid the same; to have the same perks and generally to be treated the same. In my view, that's never been the way to proceed, and like life, you'll never have a situation where all people are equal. What a dull, old world it would be if that were the case. You'll always have your star players, the people who know they can take liberties. Simply, they take liberties because they are good.

I honestly feel we have nothing to worry about. You'll always get the pessimists who say the game has never been in a worse state. I don't think it's in a bad condition at all. The knockers say look at the gates and how they've dropped off down the years. But we're living in the modern world, and the 1980s have so much to offer the punter looking for entertainment.

I tell you what, for anyone who enjoys or even loves football, they'll still go to the games that stimulate interest, where they can watch quality players having a good crack at putting on a show. Let's keep all our natural characteristics. By all means retain our aggression, our tackling, our running and the physical part of the game. I'm not saying get rid of that. Skill must be allowed to float to the top. But for goodness sake let's stop saying we ought to play like the Brazilians. We're not Brazilian – we're English, or Scottish, Irish and Welsh. We don't want to play like Brazil, Argentina or Italy – if we play it our way we can handle anyone.

There is an area where the game can improve things, like the racing industry, by providing better facilities for the public who want to come and watch. People don't want to put up with Ice Age conditions where they are paying £5 to sit out in the cold and slowly freeze in the cause of watching football. People are beginning to want comfort at football grounds. Let's be fair, a big contribution to the European Cup Heysel Stadium disaster in Brussels was the place being in poor repair, along with too many people crammed into too small a space. We're moving fast towards the twenty-first century and it's time football realized that people won't put up with ancient facilities. That's where clubs like Manchester United have got it right. They have excellent restaurants and plush surroundings – but they haven't done away with the basics that the game stands for. You can still stand on the Old Trafford terraces. They've got the balance right.

I believe there is nothing to stop the smaller clubs from following United's lead in scaled down versions, even if it means local councils helping out financially. The Crewe

Alexandras, the Tranmeres and the Halifaxes should be made into places where the local people can come and watch football in some degree of comfort – and not just football. A good friend of mine, pro-golfer Dave Allen, runs snooker clubs. Why can't we have snooker, squash and the other sports as part of our local football clubs? A football club has got to be part of the community. It will still be there a long time after Mick Channon, Kevin Keegan or Bryan Robson are gone. Football is our biggest sport, it generates great enthusiasm and brings people together. The game should be the focal point of any football club. But there should also be many other facilities incorporated in that club, to make it a family concern. A football club should be beneficial to everyone in the community. It must expand to survive. Then you will find that the local community come together more, especially for big events like the FA Cup where everyone in an area feels part of their own team. This is especially true of non-League clubs like Altrincham, famous for their FA Cup exploits. I used to live there when I played for Manchester City and the place comes alive when they go on one of their Cup runs. A little town like Altrincham may be squeezed for publicity when surrounded by the big city clubs of Manchester and Liverpool, but most years they have a big Cup win and bring people together.

If clubs can be more than just a place to watch football, they have a fair chance of keeping the interest of those people who might go along only for the big occasion. People relate to a town or city if they are born there, brought up there or live there for a certain amount of time. The trouble at a lot of non-progressive clubs lies with the directors who are often on a big ego trip. They may be trying to do their best for the club, but they want to boost themselves as well. They've got to look beyond that and make the general public welcome, because a football club within a town or city is an institution and shouldn't be allowed to die.

I am all for restructuring the League and cutting down on the divisions if necessary to make them more streamlined.

That's just as long as there is an opportunity for every humble, village green club registered with the Football Association to be able to dream of getting into the First Division – if, of course, they merit it – by climbing all the way through in a promotion system. To me it is absolutely farcical that the League for so long remained tantamount to a closed shop. It was scandalous that the club which finished top of the Gola League, the peak of non-League achievement, in the past, was not guaranteed a place in the Fourth Division. Ambition is the motivating force of any competitive footballer worth his salt. By imposing a false ceiling – like the Football League used to do on all other clubs by means of the re-election system – that ambition was cut off. If you can't aim to be the best there's not much point in playing the game.

18 · Back with Bally

The despair of failing to get promotion with Portsmouth tempts me to suggest that the only way Pompey will get back into the First Division is if there's a Third World War! They need another Adolf Hitler to threaten our shores and throw the club back into the war years when they were considered to be top notch – and they could pinch the best players from around the country simply because those stars were stationed near Portsmouth in the Navy. If you didn't look at it hilariously there would be only one thing to do – cry, in frustration.

Apart from the bitterness of missing out on promotion in the final weeks, I've had a great year with Portsmouth. Summoned by my best mate from England and Southampton days, Alan Ball, it seemed as though we had a one-way ticket to the First Division. Unfortunately we were halted one stop short of our destination.

In that crazy, up-and-down season I feel I've almost gone full circle career-wise, meeting characters at Portsmouth who were very similar to the Ale House Lads of my early days with Southampton. They play the game at Portsmouth the way *they* want to play it. In lots of ways I loved it, and in many respects it was successful because we went totally against the Establishment.

We went storming off at the top of the Second Division with a team of rejects – the bad lads of football, the mongrels that no one else wanted because of their reputations. These guys were different from any other bunch of players I have ever met: so strange and complex as individuals, but so exciting when pulled together in a team. Individually it was easy to see that they all had enough ability to be top class players, but in the end, their weaknesses, when pooled together, let them down completely.

The only discipline they recognised was their own. You couldn't bring them to heel as individuals. And at the end of a long, hard season when we had a lot of injuries and suspensions, that lack of restraint cost us promotion.

It was very sad because for the majority of the season Pompey were far and away one of the top two teams in the Second Division. Norwich, my much-loved old club, were obviously the best-disciplined side, with some exceptional players like Steve Bruce, Dave Watson, Chris Woods and Mark Barham. Having worked with their manager, Ken Brown, and coach, Mel Machin, I knew they would have no trouble in handling their team. But that's not having a dig at Alan Ball. I don't think the manager exists who could have disciplined Portsmouth. In fact, Alan Ball did an amazing job in pulling his team together and keeping the whole thing rolling when the wheels looked like falling off at any minute.

It was a tightrope that Bally was walking. If he had gone the other way and cracked down too hard on the players he could have lost six or seven of them. Then, never mind promotion, we could have been looking at the Third Division. These boys trained and worked hard, but their waywardness let them down – especially when things went wrong. That's when they wanted to fight the world.

The Pompey lads were fierce competitors who would hurl themselves at their task, quite blindly at times, but to harness all that raw passion and devilment was a massive job for anyone. All they wanted to do was win, but that obsession in every game made them vulnerable. They would charge forward, oblivious of the danger, and leave themselves open at the back. They just didn't know when to sew things up.

Some people say that Portsmouth bottled it for promotion.

Great season, shame about the outcome …

I can assure you that is one thing they would not have done, because those boys had no notion of fear. Alan Ball, John Deacon, the League or the FA couldn't induce an ounce of fear in them. 'We're going to do it *our* way,' was their shout – and they so nearly did. We either won or lost – draws were few and far between. If we'd settled for a point just a couple of times, we would have gained promotion to the First Division for sure.

At times, away from home to the likes of Grimsby and Oldham, we pulverized the opposition – pinning them in their own half. But instead of keeping things steady, we'd let them break away and score. Then it would be back up their end to command the game – but we'd end up getting beaten.

If that's a crime, I feel sorry for Alan Ball. I don't think anyone else could have handled Portsmouth's collection of wild men as well as he did. The managers I've been around and worked under would never have tolerated so many hard-to-handle players. Bally, because of his personality, managed to keep the momentum going until those last couple of weeks. It was then, when the going got tough and things were piling up against us, the players still kept throwing themselves forward. All they wanted to do was win. We simply committed suicide. I feel so sorry for Bally, and it probably cost me another season at Portsmouth. I was out on a free transfer and looking to pick up the reins again at another club.

It had all been so different at the start of the season. Everything had gone sour for me at Norwich, with relegation following our Milk Cup triumph. I was at home, after a blinding week at Goodwood races, with most clubs back into pre-season training. Suddenly the phone rang and it was Bally asking me what I was doing. 'Going racing, I think,' was my reply. I asked him if he'd heard anything that might get me another club. I said I'd have to wait and see what came up. I could have gone to Wolves as a coach, but after seeing what they went through last season, finally dropping into the Fourth Division, it was a good thing, on reflection, that I didn't end up at Molineux.

There's no doubt that when you've been a big name, and outspoken as well, people are very wary of employing you. Bally just said: 'Get your backside down here, the chairman wants to see you – you might as well come to us for a month.' Bally said he'd been trying to buy people, but clubs were asking six figures for men who couldn't play up front.

It was a situation that I had always wanted to avoid if I could. Bally is my best mate and I didn't want anything to threaten that relationship. There were people around who suggested that I might be creeping behind his back to try and get his job. But anyone who knows me will say that the last thing I'd ever try to do would be to nick someone's job, especially a mate's. It's different if someone has got the sack and you are invited to apply for a job. So although some people might have questioned my motives, they could not have been more wrong. No doubt the possibility even crossed Bally's mind at some stage, but it was never in my thoughts.

I went down to Portsmouth, saw the chairman, John Deacon, and I was in business again. It went so well that I was then asked to sign for the full season, which I did. I was a bit dubious about that because I didn't want to put Bally in a difficult situation. He knows I couldn't just play in the reserves, I'm not a reserve-team player. However, the football side of things worked out really well, apart from the last couple of months, which were really hard as I was carrying an ankle injury during that time.

So I gave it a crack, and Pompey couldn't have got off to a better start with a long unbeaten run. We were playing some terrific stuff. In the middle of our purple patch we went to Tottenham to hold them in the Milk Cup, before putting them out in the second replay down at Fratton Park. But the game at White Hart Lane wasn't our best performance of the season, it just proved what a lot of character we had. Again, we didn't know how to defend. It was a real ding-dong, and I would have scored late on – but for an incredible

Ray Clemence save – to put Spurs out of their misery straight away.

The Milk Cup should have been Spurs' best chance of winning a trophy, and if they'd managed it, Shreeve would certainly have still been in a job at Tottenham today. We murdered Aston Villa in the quarter-final, only to get let down by our normally reliable goalkeeper, Alan Knight. He threw in three goals and broke his fist into the bargain. But in extra time, against a First Division side, away from home, in the last twenty-five minutes, Alan didn't touch the ball once with his injured hand – that's how much on top we were without getting the victory we deserved. It proved the ability that we had as a Second Division side.

However, Portsmouth are *still* a Second Division side because of their discipline, or lack of it, and that crazy, win-at-all-costs attitude. I don't think they'll ever change. I hope I'm wrong, and that they can get promotion after missing out by a whisker two seasons running. I just don't know whether this team can ever realize Bally's dream of managing in the First Division. I feel that the crowd at Fratton Park are hung-up with their fathers' memories of the 1930s and late 1940s. In modern years, they have seen the bit of success that Southampton have had down the road and this has made Portsmouth's failures doubly hard to take. Portsmouth is a very tough area, like any place with docklands, and they demand success.

Bally will always go for players who can play, and will stick by them. I hold my hands up to him there. He wants his team to play the game as he played it himself, and he was top class. That's a plus, but sometimes the sad fact is that the players under you aren't as good as you were, and can't achieve what you could.

Bally and I go back to our England days under Sir Alf Ramsey. Alan was already a national hero, as one of our 1966 World Cup-winners. We became firm friends as fellow players, and it tickles me to think that I was to end up playing for him. We are completely different, opposites in lots of ways, and yet we are very similar in our approach to life.

He was a midfield player and I was a front man. I needed a service and he provided it. We disagreed fiercely at times about how games should be approached and yet, as I say, we depended on each other. We had this good understanding, both in the England team and during my second spell with Southampton.

We were friends off the pitch, going racing together, without living in each other's pockets. We loved a good laugh. We used to argue a lot about football, perhaps because if something didn't work out we could get frustrated. A classic example of our relationship came when Southampton played Tottenham at The Dell, and Ossie Ardiles had just joined the London club after being a World Cup-winning hero for Argentina. We weren't playing well, there was no spark, and after about half an hour Bally and I were scrapping, like cat and dog.

I was giving him a rollicking, telling him to start getting hold of the ball and do something with it. Bally wouldn't take that lying down, and he told me to get running about or else. The ball had gone dead and I was standing on the half-way line with Bally some fifteen yards away. I'd just had another shout at Bally and spat towards the floor, when who should walk by and catch the flow all down him but poor Ossie. What an introduction to English football for the little man. He looked so bewildered as he wiped himself down. Bally and I glanced at each other and then at Ossie, we just couldn't help laughing. The next minute Bally had knocked in a lovely through ball and I had scored to make it 1–0. We got the best out of each other. Ossie may have been right in the firing line when I spat, but that broke the tension for Bally and me.

Bally's enthusiasm was so infectious – great at getting people going – and he lasted a very long time as a player. We've sat up all night together talking football on countless occasions, and it was no surprise to me that he wanted to go into management. He's got a great knack of handling big names and people who want to play. He's knowledgeable about the game and understands the tactical side of it very well. But I felt for him in the 1985–6 season, because I thought he was on his own a bit and he didn't have someone to bounce ideas off. He took everything on the chin. That's not being detrimental to his assistant Graham Paddon, who's a smashing lad and works hard with the kids and reserves.

Bally needed someone else, like Norwich's Ken Brown has Mel Machin. Alan loves the game and it's right that he had got a good job. It's hard to believe the long hours he works, seeing kids' games in the mornings, reserve matches in the afternoons and first-team games at night. If there's a player to be checked, he would drive hundreds of miles to watch him. He does all this over four or five days a week. He's got some energy, the wee man, even at this stage of his life. His dad was a fiery sort of bloke, and Bally is very similar.

Overall, I enjoyed my season at Portsmouth. I'm as disappointed as anyone that they didn't make promotion. The club is just crying out for success. I've known the chairman, John Deacon, since I was at Southampton, and he's always been very good to me. He *is* Portsmouth in lots of ways, always digging deep in his pocket. Everything he does is from the heart and for the club. But sometimes the passion that runs through the area takes precedence over what is best when it comes to buying players. The fans demand success so much and the chairman so badly wants the club to do well that some of their signings have been too hasty. Too often the easiest way seems to buy someone to keep the supporters quiet, but that doesn't always work. However, don't let's forget they were in the Fourth Division not long ago, and the chairman has picked them up so much that they stand on the brink of the First Division. It was a club in decline long before John Deacon got involved, back in the late 1950s.

Pompey have had wobbles since Deacon took over, but he has tried to bring good players to the club, spent his own money and been positive. Whether he has done the right thing, only time will tell. Portsmouth are in desperate need of some stability right now, and I'm a great believer that things should change slowly. I've never known Bally be so disappointed, in all the time we've been together, as when Pompey didn't go up. It was the biggest thing of his life. In two years of management in the Second Division he hasn't been out of the top five, yet people were talking about him getting the sack if Portsmouth didn't make it on the second attempt. That's scandalous. I didn't think he would get the push, common sense has got to prevail. He has had success in finishing fourth two seasons running. In the 1985–6 season we weren't out of the top two until the last week, and although Charlton and Wimbledon ultimately beat us to the two promotion places behind Norwich, it was only after we'd got the better of both of them on their own grounds. Good luck to them in the First Division. I believe Wimbledon will stay up and Charlton will struggle, but neither can play, compared to Portsmouth.

Perhaps we have to look more closely at the wild bunch of players, who must take the brunt of the blame for Pompey not going up. No one has got a more fearsome image in the game than midfield man, Mick Kennedy, who is supposed to feature in more opponents' little black books than any player around. Yet I have to say that he has a tremendous attitude to the game, is a very hard trainer and he does nothing on a Saturday that he doesn't do in training, where he's smacked me on the nose with a flying elbow and sent blood spurting out. He's a very solid player who perhaps does, as they say, kick lumps out of opponents. 'What kind of an animal is he?' players have asked me after games, but I quickly point out that they don't get any different treatment than that which he hands out in training. In fact, all the Pompey lads are like that in training. I've never experienced such a physical side, and how we didn't have more injuries in training I'll never know. At Norwich we used to stop physical contact during the Friday five-a-sides before Saturday's big game: not at Portsmouth – the muzzles never go on.

Does Kennedy go too far? I don't think so. His effectiveness would be taken away if you tried to curb his aggression. In my opinion he's not as black as he's painted. He may be a little bit late at times in the tackle, but I don't think he goes over the top. There are players that do. He has an unfortunate habit of spitting that particularly upsets opponents, and I don't condone that. But I can't help liking the lad for being such a great competitor and a totally dedicated professional. He's got one thing on his mind, and that's wanting to play in the First Division. There's nothing wrong with that in my eyes. One unfortunate side-effect of Kennedy's aggressive instincts was the number of suspensions that he, and other players like him in the team, incurred. We were decimated at times by players being banned, and that didn't help us keep a settled side.

Then there was Billy Gilbert. Here you have a player who is potentially top class, but he's a lazy so-and-so. Not in his training, but he knows he's good and has never forgotten he was part of that Crystal Palace mob who were going to be the 'team of the eighties'. They were told they were great young players, and he's got that laid-back attitude that I think is stopping him fulfilling his true potential. If he were to play in a Cup Final, he would be man of the match because he'd be suitably wound up. But over forty-two League games in a season he just can't concentrate for that long. No one can take away his ability, but he just switches off and that's where you lose him.

Billy's partner in central defence, Noel Blake, has similar faults. He's prone to laziness, and always wants to be the back player and consequently puts opponents on-side. He's very stubborn and when you try and tell him something, he thinks you are having a go at him personally. Yet when you get him off the park he's one of the nicest people you could wish to meet.

I've seen some skilful black players in my time, but winger

Vince Hilaire could be out of this world. Another of that Palace team of the 1980s, Vince had a very good season when I was at Portsmouth. He has got stunning talent on the ball, although his final pass or cross often lets him down. However, he is like a lot of coloured players who, to me, seem to lack that consistency you need over a season. You put them on the pitch and you don't really know what you're going to get, so they are not always the easiest to play with. But Vince is the best black lad I can remember lining up alongside.

Our other winger, Kevin O'Callaghan, a reject from Ipswich, would be a world beater if he was half as good as he thought he was. After saying that, he has got a terrific left foot, and did have to play the last part of the 1985–6 season with a cartilage problem. He scored a lot of important goals for us – but what a whinger. To hear him carry on you would think he had invented the word 'moan'. Again he has unquestioned ability, but is inconsistent. He's a typical winger, a wayward type who will flit in and out of games. It's a nightmare for strikers when you don't know what's coming from your winger. But then again, they have to rely on getting a service themselves.

One of Pompey's midfield players, Kevin Dillon is another who in terms of skill could compete at the highest level. I know now why Pompey got all those players so cheaply, considering their high talent. The League table tells the story of a bunch of players whose personal discipline lets them down. Our goalkeeper Alan Knight, a lovely fellow who was good enough to get in the England Under-21 set-up, made too many basic mistakes in vital games. It was just plain carelessness when he did things like stepping out of his area still handling the ball. The free-kick is rifled into the net, and instead of three points you are left with one. He would also let the occasional cross float over his head into the far corner of his goal which didn't help.

In the long term, however, Bally's devotion to bringing on the kids will pay off. The young defender, Paul Hardyman, is very promising, and teenage left-back, Lee Sandford, has already made his mark on the England Youth team and could go further. Big Mick Tait may look like a bit of an agricultural player at times, but we missed him when he was out more than most people will realize. It was because of his injury trouble that we were finally pipped for promotion. He was solid, reliable and you did know what you were going to get from him.

Mick was built in the tradition of tough heroes that made the club great back in the early 1950s, like Jimmy Scoular, Harry Harris and Jimmy Dickinson. The trouble is that since those far off days Portsmouth haven't produced good enough players to replace those heroes. So people down there are still living in the past.

It wasn't easy for me to be accepted by the Portsmouth people. I'm sure a lot of them hated me when I first went there, because I'm what they call in those parts a 'scummer', someone from the rival town, Southampton, although I actually come from the Salisbury area. I have noticed that there is a terrible hatred in a lot of Portsmouth people for folk from Southampton, just twenty minutes' drive down the motorway. But funnily enough, it doesn't seem to work the other way. So there was a barrier for me to break down – although I was lucky early on that we were playing well and winning games. Yet there was still a minority who wouldn't accept me, and that ill-feeling emerged from time to time. I have to rub salt in Pompey people's wounds and remind them that Portsmouth aren't as good as Southampton. The club has been allowed to run down in the past when they didn't make the most of their success. When you think that Pompey won the League two years running in the late 1940s, it was terrible to allow the club to fall to rack and ruin, before their recent revival. The club just didn't make the most of what they had when they were a power. Success was taken for granted, the ground wasn't improved because they thought the place was too good. It's been a long, hard road back, and this latest slip-up shows they aren't there yet.

I believe that if we had achieved promotion, Portsmouth

would have had to spend out £1 million on new players – or tumbled straight back to the Second Division. More quality and more consistency costs big money. A lot of those players I have mentioned had great ability and have been with good clubs, but most of them were transferred because they had fatal flaws that were bound to show through eventually.

I always remember Lawrie McMenemey telling me that death comes quickly in this game, and he's so right. Come up with the goods, or they'll have your head off, and that's the way it should be. Out of all this I think Bally is a survivor and can come through his disappointments. He's got a bubbling personality that people will always respond to. And those lads have still played better for him than they have for their previous managers. But whether they are good enough to get where they want to be is another matter. They might not get the opportunity because their heads could well be gone.

I remember saying to Bally at Christmas 1985 that all we had to do was keep ticking over to make sure of promotion. There didn't seem any way we could fail. But I said that we ought to do away with one of the wingers and put an extra man into the middle of the park for a bit more stability. We didn't need to keep going hell for leather, we just had to be nice and solid. It may have been a bit foreign to Bally's nature, as he was still all for flying at teams' throats down both flanks. But I didn't see that we needed to take any risks. Then we ran out of midfield players, through injuries and suspensions, and we were forced to carry on playing two wingers. Another problem was that Mick Tait had to be brought out of defence to do an emergency job in midfield. All of a sudden you could see the problems starting to build. We were unable to tighten things up just when we needed to if we were to rubber-stamp promotion. A home defeat by Oldham in March was a crucial result, after we'd played pretty well and deserved something out of the game. Suddenly I thought that it was going against us and we might be in a spot of bother.

Another bad reverse came at home to Leeds, after we had led 1–0 at half-time. Bally had come in at the interval reading the riot act and saying we would get nothing out of the game. He was right. Yet we had got through crunch games well. We beat Charlton at their place, knocked over local rivals Brighton away and drew at home to Wimbledon, whom we had thrashed at Plough Lane. It was after the Leeds defeat that the feeling of impending doom was getting through to Bally. They should have been there for the taking, and I remember having a meal with him later that night. He didn't know who else he could put in the side, what with the injuries and suspensions. It was the first time that Bally expressed doubts, and told me he thought we might miss out. Unfortunately, he proved again to be dead right.

We had been good enough against the three clubs who were promoted. We beat Norwich, did the double over Charlton and took four points out of Wimbledon, but our boys had to push their self-destruct button and we fell down against moderate opposition that should have been put away. The last straw came when we had to win at Sheffield United in our last away game, to keep our faint First Division dreams alive. They weren't very good and we were just as bad. We didn't fire at all. That was one big game we couldn't handle, and we knew it was all up.

Perhaps I've been a bit critical of some of the Pompey players, it's the disappointment pouring out of me. But I did enjoy working with them. Portsmouth was one of the best experiences in my career, because I've met remarkable characters down there and I've got a much better understanding about gifted players who have fallen by the wayside.

I've had my rows with all sorts of people throughout my career – players, coaches, managers, the game's administrators, reporters, the lot – but that's because I've always been one to stand up and air my views, even though they may not be what people always want to hear. But I like to think I have helped to make the football world an interesting place down the years, and that I haven't finished ruffling a few feathers yet.

I don't want to go out on a sad note – missing promotion – and I'm determined to stay in the game playing or managing. Football has been my life and the characters in it have enriched the years. It's been totally engrossing, and if I was asked whether I wanted to change anything my answer would be 'no'. I'd do it exactly the same way all over again – and always with a smile.

Appendix

Career Statistics

		Games	Goals
Southampton (*first spell*)	*League*	392	155
	Cups	77	38
Manchester City	*League*	72	24
	Cups	22	6
Southampton (*second spell*)	*League*	119	28
	Cups	16	4
Newcastle United	*League*	4	1
Bristol Rovers	*League*	9	0
Norwich City	*League*	89	16
	Cups	23	9
Portsmouth	*League*	36	6
	Cups	4	0
England		46	21
Total		909	308